Bernard & Abelard

Sister Edmée SLG

First published in 1976
New revised edition 2024

Fairacres Publications 222

ISBN 978-0-7283-0410-9
Fairacres Publications Series ISSN 0307-1405

Edited and typeset in Palatino Linotype by Julia Craig-McFeely

Biblical quotations are taken from the Authorized King James Version of the Bible unless otherwise noted.

SLG Press
Convent of the Incarnation
Fairacres • Oxford
www.slgpress.co.uk

Printed by
Grosvenor Group Ltd, Loughton, Essex

CONTENTS

Acknowledgements ii

Introduction 1

The Emergence of 'Modern Man', 1050–1150 4

St Bernard and the Schools 12

Peter Abelard 19

The Lover 22

The Consequences of Love 26

The Thinker 35

Abelard's Writings 43

As Far as Thought Can Reach 49

Bibliography 59

ACKNOWLEDGEMENTS

This essay has been extensively revised and updated from the first edition in *The Influence of Saint Bernard: Anglican Essays with an Introduction by Jean LeClercq* OSB, Fairacres Publications 60 (SLG Press, 1976), 89–134.

We are greatly indebted to the generosity of the late Betty Radice and to Penguin Books Ltd for allowing us to quote extensively from her translation of *The Letters of Abelard and Héloïse,* first published in Penguin Classics in 1974.

Permission was also generously given for use of the following extracts:

Two passages from *Medieval Humanism and Other Studies* by Richard W. Southern, by permission of Basil Blackwell, Oxford.

Two passages from *The Evolution of Medieval Thought* by David Knowles, by permission of the Longman Group Ltd.

The passage from *The Mystical Theology of Saint Bernard* by Etienne Gilson, by permission of Sheed and Ward Ltd.

Two passages from *Saint Bernard on the Song of Songs,* translated by a Religious CSMV, by permission of A. R. Mowbray Ltd.

Biblical quotations are taken from the King James Version of the Bible.

Bernard & Abelard

Love knocks and enters; knowledge stands without.

Hugh of St Victor

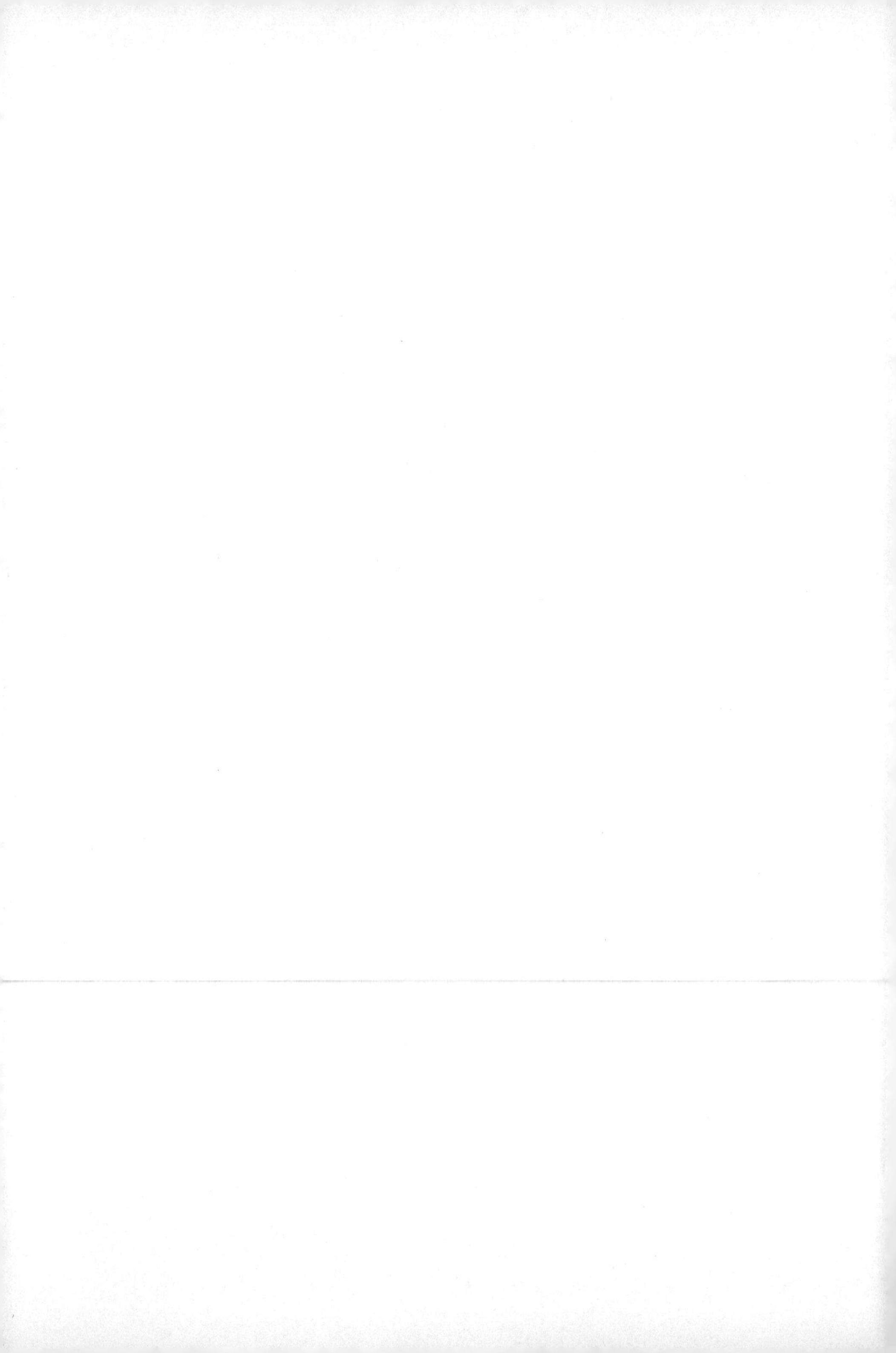

INTRODUCTION

In the centuries following his condemnation at the Council of Sens in 1140 Peter Abelard (1079–1142), although never lacking supporters among specialists, has usually been portrayed at the popular level as an arrogant if clever thinker who over-played a dangerous hand and was deservedly crushed, not a minute before time, by that champion of the true faith St Bernard of Clairvaux (1090–1153). But the rationalism and romanticism of the nineteenth century combined to alter the perspective, since when Abelard has been attracting increasing attention, both scholarly and romantic, and as, in consequence, his stock goes up so St Bernard's goes down until, in most modern studies, Bernard is presented (if more implicitly than explicitly) as the villain of the piece whose reactionary zeal cut down a veritable Socrates—'another opponent of selfdeception and loose thinking who had been misrepresented as a corrupting influence on the minds of the young'.[1]

Since Abelard's star is still waxing it would be premature to attempt to suggest, as is commonly done when opposing views are set forth, that the truth lies midway between them, even if such seemed to be the case which, to the present writer at least, it does not. There is, indeed, much truth in both extremes. But whether the balance falls in favour of Bernard or Abelard depends less, perhaps, on any objective assessment which, once made, would be available to all, but on individual capacity to apprehend the truths of doctrine. If the truths promulgated by the Church on the basis of Scripture and experience pierce to the marrow of one's being then Bernard's excitement can be

[1] Betty Radice, trans., ed. and introd., *The Letters of Abelard and Héloïse* (Penguin Classics, 1974), 42. I have relied heavily on Radice's excellent introduction and the notes to the text throughout.

shared. If they do not, but are merely intellectually conceded, which would appear by and large to be the situation nowadays among writers on the subject, then sympathy swings to Abelard, and Bernard's invective seems incomprehensible if not repellent.

It is in any case undeniable that to anyone with a contemporary temper of mind Bernard emerges from the conflict with Abelard in an unappealing light, examine the facts as one may. Moreover, even some of Bernard's contemporaries, less sentimental and with a sharper sense of the horror of heresy than ourselves, viewed his handling of the matter with disquiet. For instance, the gentle Abbot of Cluny, Peter the Venerable, unwavering admirer of Bernard as he was, rebuked him severely on this occasion and, welcoming the broken Abelard into his own monastery, insisted on him taking senior rank in the Community, absolved him on his deathbed, and sent a profoundly moving account of his last days to Héloïse, thus fulfilling in every detail the role which the world easily recognizes as that of the ideal Christian.

Yet, if Bernard's behaviour towards Abelard 'lacked his usual serenity', as one biographer mildly remarks,[2] it may, nevertheless, no more become us to criticize than for a party at the bottom of a mountain to mark a lack of detachment in someone at the top whose energetic gesticulations are attempting to convey that he or she can see a fatal danger ahead which they cannot. For, however much we may appreciate Abelard's role as questioner and underminer of the status quo, in relation to Bernard, he was a climber among the foothills, the effect of whose excursions into higher altitudes of thought on his followers was, in the long run, more deadly than bracing, as Bernard was able, with such clarity and urgent sense of alarm, to see they would prove to be.

As for Bernard in relation to Abelard, it has become customary to call him a traditionalist. But even if one allows the appellation it is

[2] Bruno Scott James, *Saint Bernard of Clairvaux: An Essay in Biography* (Hodder & Stoughton, 1957), 139.

a misleading one to us, giving rise to semi-conscious associations of a derogatory kind which do little justice to the power and originality of Bernard's genius. It would be more accurate, if less brief, to say that he trod the straight and narrow way of which Christ himself said 'few there be that find it' (Matt. 7:14).

THE EMERGENCE OF 'MODERN MAN' 1050–1150

> And the children struggled together within her ... And the LORD said unto her, Two nations *are* in thy womb, and two manner of people shall be separated from thy bowels; and *the one* people shall be stronger than *the other* people; and the elder shall serve the younger.
>
> The birth of Esau and Jacob (Gen. 25:22–3)

Current scholarship is disinclined to give credence to the once-held view that Christendom expected dissolution as it approached the year 999 and surged forward with relief into the year 1001,[3] although R. W. Southern in his essay 'Medieval Humanism' indicates just such a view when he notes a result of it and concludes: 'Then quite suddenly the terror faded and the sun shone.'[4] Certainly much of the evidence continues to be susceptible of the 'day of judgement' interpretation—neither need we laugh. 'Are we prepared to meet our doom?' asked the *Sunday Times* in a leading article (24 November 1974) typical of the prevailing mood, which described a religious community in Germany which is refusing postulants in expectation of the imminent end of the world and circulated a news-sheet not long ago headed 'Countdown to disaster', its contents including a full catalogue of prophecies, belongs to twentieth- not tenth-century history. This latter example may seem too freakish for notice but future historians will

[3] Cf. David Knowles, *The Evolution of Medieval Thought* (Longmans, 1962), 79.

[4] Richard W. Southern, *Medieval Humanism and Other Studies* (Harper Torchbook, 1970), 35. The essay 'Medieval Humanism' brilliantly illuminates that subject and remains for me by far the best work I have read on it.

doubtless hold it up to the light as symptomatic of our expectations of dissolution, gathering gloomily in today's world.

The difference between then and now is the difference of direction from which the day of judgement is expected. Then it was expected from God. Now it is expected from humanity. And this change is the logical consequence of that change in the eleventh century when people stopped riveting their attention on God, as someone in the dock for murder might rivet their attention on the judge as sentence is about to be pronounced, and return it to their natural centre of attention, themselves, when a reprieve has been granted. Southern, in the essay referred to above, describes how it was before 1050:

> In the main tradition of the early Middle Ages nearly all the order and dignity in the world was closely associated with supernatural power. There was order in symbolism and ritual, and order in worship and sacrament, and both of them were elaborate and impressive. Man's links with the supernatural gave his life a framework of order and dignity; but in the natural order the chaos was almost complete. Almost nothing was known about secondary causes in natural event. Rational procedures in law, in government, in medicine, in argument, were scarcely understood or practised even in the most elementary way. Man chiefly knew himself as a vehicle for divine activity. There was a profound sense of the littleness and sinfulness of man. Both physically and mentally human life had narrow limits: only in prayer and penance, in clinging to the saints, was there any enlargement. Man was an abject being, except when he was clad in symbolic garments, performing symbolic and sacramental acts, and holding in his hands the earthly remains of those who already belonged to the spiritual world. ... Perhaps this awe-struck, sacramental view of man's place and powerlessness in the world gives a more satisfactory account of man's situation in the universe than the optimism of the succeeding centuries; and optimism never overcame the final impotence of man and his need for supernatural aid. But there is a sharp change of emphasis after about 1050.[5]

[5] Southern, *Medieval Humanism*, 32f.

Southern goes on to say that the first signs of the change were to be seen in the monasteries where it 'took the form of a greater concentration on man and on human experience as a means of knowing God', and that one of its most significant moments occurred in Normandy in 1079:

> In this year Anselm at Bec entered into the chamber of his mind, excluded everything but the word 'God' and found that suddenly the word articulated itself into a demonstration of God's existence, which he believed to be both new and true. It was new, and whether or not it was true, it was a triumph of an analytical introspective method. It seemed to show that men could find new truths of the greatest general importance simply by looking within themselves. The idea of finding something new was itself new to a generation which had believed itself to be at the end of the road; and to find the new things so close at hand, and so entirely central, was a revelation of the powers that lay within man's mind.[6]

But the revelation of the powers that lie within the human mind are only wholly safe in the hands of a saint. The same year, 1079, saw the birth of Abelard, intellectually the heir of St Anselm, but in whom spiritual stature was already to degenerate into psychological type. Then in 1090 Bernard, another heir to Anselm, was born who, says Southern, popularized the method of introspection and made it the property of a school of monastic writers, giving the whole exercise a new direction, while not interested, as Anselm had been, in logic and analysis but only in spiritual growth.[7]

Abelard, on the other hand, was only interested in logic and analysis and not at all in spiritual growth, and so we see that by the beginning of the twelfth century a division of Anselm's patrimony had taken place. What had been unified in him, and had thus begun in a certain state of perfection, as new movements generally do, now divided and began to develop independently and at many levels.

---

[6] Southern, *Medieval Humanism*, 33.

[7] Southern, *Medieval Humanism*, 34.

The elder son, so to speak, cultivated and brought under control the external world, whether in learning, as it developed in the Schools, or in the first stirrings of scientific discoveries. Chenu says that 'the rise of technology surpassed quantitatively and qualitatively the still-elementary awareness that professional and religious people had of the role technology was to play', and among technological advances he lists: the perfecting of machines to harness waterpower and to produce circular motion; mill wheels; hydraulic wheels, which enabled one horse to do the work that formerly required twenty-five; windmills, first used in Europe in 1105; machines that could store power through a system of weights and geared wheels; new armaments that made the old mounted warrior obsolete; new means of transport and travel, giving men increased freedom; the invention of the draft collar for horses and oxen which transformed rural life; and—neither last nor least—the mechanical clock which, says Chenu, 'began to rationalize time, its regularity measuring out a mechanized civilization ... The new gadget was everywhere and cast a new aura round existence which was governed now not by rhythms natural to human life but by a mechanical time'. He goes on to say:

> In this mechanism-minded world, man moved away from a confused trial-and-error approach, became objective and impersonal in his efforts, and grew aware of the complex structures of realities governed by natural laws. Order was no longer merely the scheme proposed by aesthetic imagination or religious conviction; it was experimentally ascertained and systematically verified, for nature was seen as penetrable and predictable ... Henceforth, the new *homo artifex,* maker of shapes and forms, distinguished between the animate and the mechanical, rid himself of the childish fancies of animism and of the habit of seeing divinity in the marvels of nature. The sacred realm which he secularized by this process no longer possessed any properly religious value for him. He knew its place in the universe better than that.[8]

---

[8] Marie-Dominique Chenu OP, *Nature, Man and Society in the Twelfth Century* (University of Chicago Press, 1968), 43–5.

Of course, humanity did not rid itself of 'the childish fancies of animism' overnight, nor did it accomplish the secularization of the sacred realm of nature in a year or two. The whole business of coming to 'know better' has, in fact, taken us from then until now—with what results the ecologists of the world, dressed as it were, in sackcloth and ashes, are now repenting. 'Thou turnest man to destruction', says the Psalmist in a mysterious phrase, and goes on: 'and sayest, Return, ye children of men. For a thousand years in thy sight are but as yesterday' (Ps. 90:3–4).

At the intellectual level the cultivation and bringing under control of the external world expressed itself in a sudden passion for learning. Whereas in 1050 education had been hardly come by, if at all, by the beginning of the 1100s there were schools everywhere. There had, indeed, been provision made for them, laid down in various documents from the time of Charlemagne in the eighth century, and although the facilities for education thus provided in theory were not normally available in practice, the consciousness that they ought to be, kept enough of a spark alive in cathedrals and parishes to enable the fire to spread rapidly when it did get going. Guibert of Nogent, who was born in 1053, tells us in his autobiography of the difficulty of finding teachers in his childhood, but by the time Abelard was born in 1079, and Bernard eleven years later, learning had not only spread to every spot where there were students to imbibe it but was of a standard beyond anything that could have been foreseen from the intellectual barrenness of the preceding centuries. Learning had, of course, been available in the monastic communities—at the price of becoming a religious—but the educated lay person was, in both senses, exceptional. By 1070 the situation was already noticeably different and thereafter accelerated so that boys of the upper classes who, like Abelard and Bernard, showed signs of intellectual capacity, were sent off to one of the new schools to get a thorough grounding in grammar, rhetoric, dialectic, and the Latin authors instead of being confined to the customary pursuits of fighting and hunting. 'Nothing indeed', says David Knowles, 'is a more impressive testimony to the widespread literary culture of the early twelfth century than the emergence of a Bernard from a small provincial school.'[9]

But if Bernard was, providentially, able to take advantage of the facilities provided by the new age, Abelard actually represented it. Bernard was intended by his parents for the Church and thus his learning, first by them and later by himself, was never regarded as more than a means to an end. In Abelard's case the emphasis was always on learning for its own sake, as the opening paragraphs of his autobiography show:

> My father had acquired some knowledge of letters before he was a soldier, and later on his passion for learning was such that he intended all his sons to have instruction in letters before they were trained to arms. His purpose was fulfilled. I was his firstborn, and being specially dear to him had the greatest care taken over my education. For my part, the more rapid and easy my progress in my studies, the more eagerly I applied myself, until I was so carried away by my love of learning that I renounced the glory of a soldier's life, made over my inheritance and rights of the eldest son to my brothers, and withdrew from the court of Mars in order to kneel at the feet of Minerva. I preferred the weapons of dialectic to all the other teachings of philosophy, and armed with these I chose the conflicts of disputation instead of the trophies of war. I began to travel about in several provinces disputing, like a true peripatetic philosopher, wherever I had heard there was keen interest in the art of dialectic.[10]

Peripatetic, meaning 'one who walks about', was the name given to the followers of Aristotle from the circumstance that he taught in the portico *(peripatos* = 'for walking about') of the Lyceum at Athens. A meaningful etymology for, as Abelard shows, the peripatetic philosophers of the twelfth century did indeed walk about, 'seeking whom they might devour' in debate.[11] Their method was

---

[9] Knowles, *Evolution of Medieval Thought*, 147.

[10] *Historia Calamitatum* in Radice, *The Letters of Abelard and Héloïse*, 57–8. All references to the *Historia Calamitatum* are to Radice's translation.

[11] Cf. 1 Pet. 5:8.

based on a structure of question *(quaestio)*, argument *(disputatio)*, and conclusion *(sententia)*, namely, posing, discussing, and resolving problems by means of question and answer, and was quite new when Abelard adopted it. The traditional manner of teaching had been to expound passages of Scripture by means of appropriate glosses and commentaries—imposed, no doubt, upon them. One visualizes a somewhat ponderous teacher, lecturing to silent, respectful, and unquestioning students. It is not surprising, then, that the entry of the peripatetic philosopher, 'more subtle than any beast of the field'—not to mention any master in the schools, according to Abelard's account—enlivened learning with his stimulatingly conversational approach: 'Did God say … ?'.[12]

In the cathedral of St Lazare at Autun, just a few miles from Clairvaux, and contemporaneously with ten years of Bernard's abbacy, the genius of Gislebertus was at work (*c.* 1125–1135) carving out in stone a pictorial representation of the beliefs and ideas of his times. 'There is little doubt that Gislebertus wished to convey a moral message in his sculpture; in fact, he was closer in spirit to St Bernard than any other sculptor of the twelfth century.'[13] Yet, close in space and spirit though he may have been, his figure of Eve sums up with a wonderful sympathy and fascination, and with not the slightest hint of a moral message, the delight men and women were experiencing in tasting afresh of the tree of knowledge. Reclining in a horizontal position, suggestive of the new age as against the old which had been vertically orientated, or perhaps because Eve always symbolizes the horizontal, she is calling men from behind a cupped hand to the feast of reason, her own eyes already wide open as the serpent had promised:

> For God doth know that in the day ye eat thereof, then your eyes shall be opened, and ye shall be as gods, knowing good and evil.
>
> (Gen. 3:5)

[12] An allusion to the serpent in Gen. 3:1–2.

[13] Denis Grivot and George Zarnecki, *Gislebertus: Sculptor of Autun* (Orion Press, 1961), 77.

All around her in the cathedral are figures who have achieved their destiny: the contemplative tranquillity of the blessed side by side with the terrifying monstrosity of the damned, each on their way to the eternal habitations of heaven or hell. But Eve is still in the process of achieving; no judgement has yet been passed on her. Meanwhile, as Scripture calls her, and as Gislebertus so marvellously conveys, she is 'the mother of all the living'.

There was, however, at that time an actual, not a figurative mother who, at one of those crucial moments of choice which affect the whole course of a life, influenced her son against the call of Eve, thus providing the Church with the greatest counterpoint figure of the age.

St Bernard and the Schools

> Everyone said that he was a youth with great prospects, and if externals were anything to judge by, he must have been; for his body was well proportioned, his face pleasing, his manner gentle and courteous, his mind keen, and his speech persuasive and appealing. Many careers in the world lay open to him, and success seemed assured in whatever he would decide to do.
>
> William of St Thierry[14]

Success hardly seemed assured, however, when Bernard decided to enter the monastery at Cîteaux, a small, struggling community, founded only fifteen years earlier and already showing signs of closing down through want of vocations, lack of perseverance among many of the founding brethren, and a number of deaths due to unhealthy conditions and undernourishment.

Bernard's family had no objection to his becoming a monk. But they had every objection to him becoming a monk at Cîteaux instead of in one of the comfortable Cluniac houses in the neighbourhood where they could have kept up contact and, no doubt, catered for

---

[14] From the *Vita Prima Sancti Bernardi Claraevallis Abbatis,* English translation in *St Bernard of Clairvaux: The Story of His Life as Recorded in the Vita Prima Bernardi ...,* trans. by Geoffrey Webb and Adrian Walker (Mowbray, 1960), 20 (henceforth *Vita Prima).* The First Life of Bernard of Clairvaux, traditionally known as the *Vita Prima,* originated to prepare the case for canonization of Bernard, first abbot of Clairvaux. The work was begun by William of Saint-Thierry, continued by Arnold of Bonneval, and completed by Geoffrey of Auxerre. When the initial case for the canonization of Bernard was rejected by Innocent II, Geoffrey undertook a revision of the original *Vita* (Recension A) and submitted another version (Recension B) to Pope Alexander III, who declared Bernard a saint in 1174.

those little extras which even the best establishments are liable to lack. Bernard himself later wrote: 'I chose Cîteaux in preference to Cluny not because I was not aware that the life was excellent and lawful but because "I am a thing of flesh and blood, sold unto the slavery of sin." [Rom. 7:14] I was conscious that my weak character needed a strong medicine.'[15]

But decisions which have to last a whole life must be made by the whole being and it seems that at first Bernard's decision to become a Cistercian, based as it was on reason and self-knowledge of the highest order, did not yet encompass his entire being. The cord which kept him bound was precisely that desire for learning which was affecting the men of his world with such force. Because of it his family were able to persuade him to go to Germany for further studies before committing himself to Cîteaux. The extent to which this plan was in accord with Bernard's literary ambitions is revealed by the violence with which he subsequently reacted against those ambitions. But while still pursuing them William of St Thierry tells us that the memory of his holy mother, Aleth, who had died in 1104 when Bernard was fourteen, began to fill his mind 'so that he seemed to see her coming to him, reproaching and upbraiding him that she had not brought him up with such love and care so that he could adopt this empty kind of existence, and that it was not for the fulfilment of such worldly ambitions that she had brought him into the world'.[16]

The crucial moment of choice came when, during the first stage of his journey, he was so disquieted by these thoughts that he stopped and, entering a church, gave himself to prayer. 'If therefore thine eye be single, thy whole body shall be full of light' (Matt. 6:22), and from thenceforth Bernard was possessed of the single eye of the true monk, emerging not only full of light but, as William of St Thierry says, 'like the flame which turns the forest into a roaring blaze and then goes on

[15] Quoted in James, *Saint Bernard of Clairvaux*, 23.
[16] *Vita Prima*, 24.

to burn the mountains black'[17]—the first victims of the blaze being the twenty-nine relations and friends whom he led on to Cîteaux within a few months.

The recruitment of this company, which included four out of five of Bernard's brothers (the fifth being too young—the only impediment permitted by Bernard—but inevitably joining him as soon as he was old enough), and their arrival at the monastery, where one pictures an abbot interrupted in his melancholy task of winding up the place with the news that thirty young men were without desiring admittance to the life,[18] makes for a story of fairy-tale timelessness. In fact, when seen against the rise of the schools, it takes on a meaning which suggests an absolute if invisible dependence of one situation upon the other. For, as it is said that wherever stinging nettles grow there also will be found a healing dock leaf, so this company of young men can be seen as forming the spearhead of a movement from which the antidote to what was pernicious in the passion for learning might be applied to society. Or, as the monks themselves understood the matter, 'whose presence, acting like leaven, worked through the whole lump and kept it from corruption'.[19]

Three years after his entry into Cîteaux Bernard was sent by his abbot, Stephen Harding, to establish Clairvaux, and this foundation in turn produced sixty-five daughter houses before the end of Bernard's life, while Cîteaux itself continued to found houses at an incredible rate. It was 'schools against schools', as Gilson says in a passage the whole of which is an admirable summary of the thought of the time:

---

[17] *Vita Prima*, 25.

[18] St Stephen Harding, the remarkable Englishman who helped to found Cîteaux, and framed the Cistercian constitution, was the abbot at this time. It is likely, in fact, that he was aware of the approaching invasion, for Bernard's fame as a recruiting agent for Cîteaux became such that, according to the *Vita Prima*, 'mothers hid their sons when Bernard came near, and wives clung to their husbands ...' (p. 32).

[19] From the chapter 'Schola Caritatis' in Etienne Gilson, *The Mystical Theology of Saint Bernard* (Sheed and Ward, 1940), 60ff.

No one, even in the twelfth century, entertained any naive illusion about a primitive Church in which all the members were perfect Christians. The number of the saints had always been small. The Gospel, since it was preached to all the world, had never been received save in the measure of the capacity of the recipients; but it was precisely on that account that even from the earliest days there was formed a small inner group of perfect imitators of Christ, whose presence, acting like a leaven, worked through the whole lump and kept it from corruption. Immediately after the death of Christ the Apostles themselves would seem to have formed a group of this kind, that is to say a school of masters whose very life was a lesson, who, for the rest, taught nothing save the Gospel offered to all, and whom few nevertheless cared to join precisely on account of the rigorous way in which they put its teachings into practice; 'and they were all with one accord in Solomon's Porch. And of the rest durst no man join himself to them: but the people magnified them' (Acts 5:12–13). These then were the first monks, and from their example we learn what from the first had always been the meaning of the monastic life:—that is, the life of an elite who, by preaching and by example, maintain the full spirit of the Gospel in a world unable to bear it.

The name attached to this group by the author of the Cistercian *Exordium* is typically Benedictine: it is a school, the School of the Primitive Church. Already at the outset of his Rule, St Benedict had proclaimed that he intended to open a school of the service of the Lord. The Cistercians had many good reasons of their own for adopting the expression and investing it with new significance. Twelfth-century France was filled with schools of profane science and ancient letters. There was not only Saint-Vories, where the young Bernard had pursued his studies with a programme that might well astonish, not to say disquiet, a soul so eager for Christ, there were Paris, Reims, Laon, Chartres—so many other famous names but always the same masters: Cicero, Virgil, Ovid, Horace, eloquent spokesmen of a world that had never read the Gospel. Why not invoke another master, the only master who has the words of eternal life? ... Cîteaux, Clairvaux and Signy were then to stand over against Reims, Laon, Paris and Chartres, schools against schools, and to vindicate in a Christian land the rights of a teaching more Christian than that with which the minds of guileless youths were wont to be poisoned.[20]

But the most powerful spokesmen of a world that had never read the Gospel were Plato and Aristotle. Cicero and the rest may have formed minds and thus to a considerable extent influenced behaviour, but Plato and Aristotle struck at the roots of being. Life looked different, *was* different when studied through those great eyes—and now suddenly it was. 'This change was not occasioned by any discovery of ancient texts', says Knowles. 'The works of Boethius ... had always been available, but whereas in the past they had evoked no response in the minds of their readers, they were now appreciated in all their dynamic force.'[21]

Just how dynamic those forces were may be seen on the one hand in the revival of Aristotelian dialectic—which produced the peripatetic philosophers—and on the other hand in the all-pervasiveness of an adapted Platonic mysticism. That mysticism inspired not only most of the religious literature of the times but issued in the great masterpieces of Gothic architecture, thus realizing in Christendom an aesthetic which held the field in art and music down to the eighteenth century.

The twelfth century, then, saw a new and universal ascendance of the two Greek minds arising solely out of its own psychology and not as a result of the arrival of fresh texts—as was to happen in the next century. Coleridge thought that each of us is from birth either a Platonist or an Aristotelian,[22] and had he been referring to the twelfth century he would perhaps have been right; for one has the impression that everybody was at that time a Greek of one kind or another. Everybody, that is, except Bernard—and he was a Hebrew of the

[20] *The Mystical Theology of Saint Bernard*, 60ff.

[21] From the chapter 'The Revival of Dialectic' in Knowles, *Evolution of Medieval Thought*, 93.

[22] From his *Table Talk* for 2 July, 1830. Harry Nelson Coleridge, ed., *Specimens of the Table Talk of the Late Samuel Taylor Coleridge*, 2 vols. (John Murray, 1835).

Hebrews. This is, of course, an immense over-simplification. In fact the structure and character of twelfth-century society was rigidly Judaic. Neither is it possible to confine even the individual to one type or another. Abelard himself exemplifies the situation: an Aristotelian 'Greek' in regard to ideas; a 'Jew' in regard to morality. Abbot Suger, on the other hand, might be said to have been an Aristotelian at the practical level, a Platonist at the aesthetic level and, finally (after his conversion under the influence of St Bernard), a Jew at the spiritual level. Nevertheless, the simplification, I think, stands, and suggests why someone like Rupert of Deutz, a biblical mystic on the Hebraic side, although involved in a number of central controversies, made no impression on the times and felt himself to be out of tune with them.

The real division in human types is between Jew and Greek, with the Platonic and Aristotelian psychologies forming a sub-division of the latter. Bernard, alone among the giants of the time, represents the 'Jew' type, which explains why to the Greek cast of mind he sticks out from the century like a sore thumb. But 'salvation is of the Jews' (John 4:22), and it is not too much to say that Bernard was raised up in the providence of God to save the brilliant opening of a new era for the Gospel, and to check the excesses into which our excitement with new knowledge inevitably leads us:

> You must not think that I am scoffing at knowledge or blaming the learned and forbidding the study of letters! [he said to his monks] Far from it! I know well what service her scholars have rendered and are rendering to the Church, both by refuting her enemies and by instructing the simple. But it is written that 'knowledge puffeth up,' while in another place, 'He that addeth knowledge addeth also grief.' There is a difference, you see, between these two: one knowledge fills a man with pride, the other saddens him. And obviously the latter is that which ministers to our salvation, for God heals the broken-hearted but abhors the proud. All knowledge which is founded on the truth is indeed good in itself. But you, who are set on working out your salvation with fear and trembling, and with all speed, because the time is short, must give priority to the studies which most nearly concern it. Doctors tell us—do they not?—that

part of the art of medicine consists in knowing what food should be taken, and in what order and manner they are best consumed. For though all foods God has created are good in themselves, you may easily make them far from good *for you* if you do not take them in the proper order and the proper way. And the same applies to the various branches of knowledge.

But I had better send you to the master, for this teaching is not ours but his ... 'If any man,' he says, 'thinks that he knows anything, he does not yet know it as he ought to know.' It is the manner of knowing that he singles out as the important thing; and that includes the order of our study, the effort we devote to it, and the end we have in view in undertaking it. As to the order, that must come first which will forward our salvation; as to the effort, the most must be expended on the studies that kindle us to love; and as to the object that we have in view, we must seek to acquire knowledge, not from vainglory or curiosity or anything like that, but only for the sake of our own edification or that of our neighbour. For there are some who desire knowledge merely for its own sake; and that is shameful curiosity. And there are others who desire to know in order that they may themselves be known; and that is vanity, disgraceful too. Others, again, desire knowledge in order to acquire money or preferment by it; that too is a discreditable quest. But there are also some who desire knowledge that they may build up others' souls with it; and that is charity. Others again, desire it that they themselves may be built up thereby; and that is prudence.

Out of all these types, the last two only put knowledge to right use. All the others merely illustrate the truth of the Apostle's saying that 'knowledge puffeth up'.[23]

[23] *Saint Bernard on the Song of Songs,* trans. and ed. by a Religious of CSMV (A. R. Mowbray, 1952), 107f. (Sermon 36).

PETER ABELARD

> At last I came to Paris, where dialectic had long been particularly flourishing, and joined William of Champeaux who at the time was the supreme master of the subject, both in reputation and in fact. I stayed in his school for a time, but though he welcomed me at first he soon took a violent dislike to. me because I set out to refute some of his arguments and frequently reasoned against him. 'On several occasions I proved myself his superior in debate ... This was the beginning of the misfortunes which have dogged me to this day, and as my reputation grew, so other men's jealousy was aroused.[24]

Thus reads the third paragraph of Abelard's 'Letter of consolation to his friend', traditionally entitled *Historia Calamitatum.* He goes on to describe how he subsequently forced William to abandon his position on the question of 'universals', and hounds him, through several pages, into a monastery where, licking his wounds and gnashing his teeth with envy, he remained, having lost hope of future worldly fame in the face of Abelard's greater brilliance. Other contemporary accounts reveal William as a saintly character. No doubt Abelard contributed greatly to his sanctification.

The next subject of attack is the famous Master Anselm of Laon who, according to Abelard, became equally consumed with jealousy, even losing his head and forbidding Abelard to continue his work of interpretation in the place where he [Anselm] taught—'an act of sheer spite and calumny such as had never been directed at anyone before'. Abelard then settled in Paris and taught for several years in the school of Notre Dame:

---

[24] *Historia Calamitatum*, 58.

> As soon as I began my course of teaching I set myself to complete the commentaries on Ezekiel which I had started at Laon. These proved so popular with their readers that they judged my reputation to stand as high for my interpretation of Scripture as it had previously done for philosophy. The numbers in the school increased enormously as the students gathered there eager for instruction in both subjects, and the wealth and fame this brought me must be well known to you.[25]

In a course of lectures, 'Abelard, his Friends and his Enemies', given by Richard W. Southern in Oxford in 1975, Southern presented a view of Anselm of Laon as a revolutionary who succeeded by virtue of his dullness in introducing the study of the Bible into the secular curriculum—a view which was itself revolutionary. This suggests that Anselm's rage with Abelard was due not to jealousy—as Abelard inevitably thought—but to his fear that Abelard's provocative handling of the new method would jeopardize what he, Anselm, had carefully rendered safe over many years of patient work. But Anselm had had a long run on a low light, so to speak, and it was inevitable that an Abelard should emerge from the pot to blow the lid off. Southern concluded his lectures by saying that Abelard's 'chief service was that he drew on himself all the hostility directed at the whole scholastic enterprise'.[26]

All this provides a strong contrast to Bernard's view that the acquisition of knowledge is only rightly undertaken in the causes of charity and prudence—two qualities conspicuously lacking in Abelard. Neither is he better endowed with the two kinds of knowledge required by Bernard: self-knowledge, leading to the knowledge of God. For the *Historia Calamitatum* exemplifies the fact that self-revelation is not only not the same as self-knowledge but may even be inimical to it, although candour certainly coincides with truth in his next paragraph:

---

[25] *Historia Calamitatum*, 65.

[26] I am deeply indebted to Sister Benedicta Ward SLG for the detailed notes she took of these lectures on my behalf. I have referred to them constantly.

Success always puffs up fools with pride, and worldly security weakens the spirit's resolution and easily destroys it through carnal temptations. I began to think myself the only philosopher in the world, with nothing to fear from anyone, and so I yielded to the lusts of the flesh.

The Lover

Abelard was about thirty-eight when, having been hitherto, as he tells us, entirely continent, the energy which had animated his intellect until then now began to slip and to animate him, as it were, whence it had arisen. To meet this new situation he resolved to take a mistress and, circumstances providentially placing in his care the young Héloïse, he decided to bring her to his bed, confident that he should have easy success. 'For', he goes on, 'at that time I had youth and exceptional good looks as well as my great reputation to recommend me, and I feared no rebuff from any woman I might choose to honour with my love.'[27]

This is a brave style for a man whose single essay into the lists of love was to unseat and enslave him so humiliatingly for, far from being in control of the situation the situation immediately took control of him and his infatuation became obsessive, with disastrous consequences on his career:

> It became utterly boring for me to have to go to the school, and equally wearisome to remain there and to spend my days on study when my nights were sleepless with love-making. As my interest and concentration flagged, my lectures lacked all inspiration and were merely repetitive; I could do no more than repeat what had been said long ago, and when inspiration did come to me, it was for writing love-songs, not the secrets of philosophy.[28]

For a man whose primary passion lay in learning, and the life which went with it, he found himself in a fearful impasse. The more he must have desired to be free from the secondary passion for Héloïse the more helplessly enmeshed he became.

---

[27] *Historia Calamitatum*, 66.

[28] *Historia Calamitatum*, 68.

And so began a series of futile efforts to free himself, which can be seen as the inevitable consequence of his belief in goodness as example and not as indwelling. In other words, his weapons in the struggle were all external to him and when they failed—as one by one they did—he could turn to nothing within, since he knew of nothing within, and was unable to hope that the victory of him who 'was in all points tempted like as we are, yet without sin' (Heb. 4:15) could save him. And, lacking that hope, liberation, for him, lay only in that which actually occurred.

His first major step in the struggle to free himself from what he later described as the 'depths of shame to which my unbridled lust had consigned our bodies, until no reverence for decency or for God, even during the days of Our Lord's Passion, or of the greater sacraments, could keep me from wallowing in this mire',[29] was to resolve upon marrying Héloïse. He evidently hoped, by being united to Héloïse in the sacred relationship of marriage, to cool the ardour which a clandestine situation inevitably fans. But as the morality of the times preferred celibacy in its teachers, he would have lost face had the marriage been known and so he insisted on it being kept secret, thus losing the benefit of freedom from 'unbridled lust' which can reasonably be expected as the reward of undertaking the marriage bond.

Héloïse understood at once the implications of this decision and resisted it with all possible force. With unblinking vanity Abelard repeats the arguments she brought against it (those which appealed to him, that is. She apparently had others,[30] about which, after reading the *Historia,* she accused him of keeping silent):

> What honour could she win, she protested, from a marriage which would dishonour me and humiliate us both? The world would justly exact punishment from her if she removed such a light from its midst. Think of the curses, the loss to the Church and grief of philosophers which would greet such a marriage! Nature had created

[29] Letter 4, Radice, *Letters of Abelard and Héloïse,* 147.

[30] See Letter 1, Radice, *Letters of Abelard and Héloïse,* 114.

> *me* for all mankind—it would be a sorry scandal if I should bind myself to a single woman and submit to such base servitude. She absolutely rejected this marriage, it would be nothing but a disgrace and a burden to me. Along with the loss of my reputation she put before me the difficulties of marriage ...

Abelard himself puts this before the reader for the next three and a half pages concluding with:

> But at last she saw that her attempts to dissuade me were making no impression on my foolish obstinacy, and she could not bear to offend *me;* so amidst deep sighs and tears she ended in these words: '*We* shall both be destroyed. All that is left us is suffering as great as our love has been.' In this, as the whole world knows, she showed herself a true prophet.[31]

Indeed, for then their troubles really began—to the pained surprise of the propounder of the ethic of pure intention.

Their meetings became increasingly few and furtive. Before the marriage Abelard had not been afraid to have a mistress but now he was fearful of it being known that he had a wife. So Fulbert, Héloïse's guardian (allegedly her uncle but fulfilling a role in the drama which suggests—beyond doubt in my view—that he was in fact her father), began to spread the news of the secret marriage and was enraged when Héloïse denied it. At this point Abelard removed her to the convent at Argenteuil where she had been brought up and, quite inexplicably on the face of it, had her dressed in the religious habit. What was his motive?

As far as I am aware no attention has been paid to this significant fact, and yet it seems worth noticing. For here, in this unremarked detail, we find confirmation in his actions of the defects in his thought. By placing Héloïse in a consecrated place and dressing her in the externals of a consecrated life he evidently intended to render her—who was his wife—untouchable, the obverse of that error of which St Paul speaks: 'he that eateth and drinketh unworthily, eateth

[31] *Historia Calamitatum*, 74.

and drinketh damnation to himself, not discerning the Lord's body' (1 Cor. 11:29). That is to say, those who put their trust in the externals of religion, failing to discern, and so to correspond with the inner reality, will be damned by those very things they hope will save them.

And so it was. Fulbert, whose perceptions had apparently been sharpened by suffering, interpreted this action as Abelard's easy way of ridding himself of Héloïse by making her a nun, and prepared his revenge.[32] Meanwhile Héloïse meditated on the Bible in her convent and Abelard expounded it in his school. His efforts at self-liberation seemed to be working. The *mise en scène* was complete. The axe, so to speak, was ready to fall. And for Abelard it finally fell on the occasion he visited Héloïse:

> You know what my uncontrollable desire did with you there, actually in a corner of the refectory, since *we* had nowhere *else* to go. I repeat, you know how shamelessly *we* behaved on that occasion in so hallowed a place, dedicated to the most holy Virgin. Even if our other shameful behaviour was ended, this alone would deserve far heavier punishment ...[33]

[32] *Historia Calamitatum*, 75.

[33] Letter 4, Radice, *Letters of Abelard and Héloïse*, 146.

The Consequences of Love

> By thy great wisdom and by thy traffick hast thou increased thy riches, and thine heart is lifted up because of thy riches: Therefore, thus saith the Lord God: Because thou hast set thine heart as the heart of God; Behold, therefore I will bring strangers upon thee, the terrible of the nations: and they shall draw their swords against the beauty of thy wisdom, and they shall defile thy brightness.
>
> (Ezek. 28:5–7)

Writers on Abelard have remained mostly silent in face of the appalling personal disaster of his mutilation, some indeed so silent that in otherwise full accounts of him they have not even mentioned it. But usually it is treated as a separate theme: Abelard the thinker on the one hand; Abelard the lover on the other. In either case it is seen as an isolated event, the consequence of an interruption of passion into his otherwise exclusively cerebral career, terrible to contemplate, yet unrelated to the significance of his life as a whole.

In this section I shall, on the contrary, suggest that the castration of Abelard is central to his psychology, and that if one places it thus instead of at the periphery, his life takes on a meaning which illuminates the case of a person as they begin to develop independently of the Creator. As we have seen, this independent development began at the turn of the eleventh century and had reached the point of establishing itself by the time Abelard came to represent it. Viewed in this light; Abelard is seen to stand at the dawn of our millennium as symbol of our ultimate impotence. He thus takes on a character of biblical dimensions, another Esau who, having renounced his birthright, is left to live by the sword (Gen. 17:40), that is, the two-edged sword of truth which cuts both ways and of which, when wielded on its own merits and in its own strength, our Lord said that 'they that take the sword shall perish with the sword' (Matt. 26:52).

My thesis, then, is that the cause of Abelard's castration lay not in his liaison with Héloïse but in the attitude of mind exemplified by the following passage:

> One day it happened that after a session of *Sentences* we students were joking amongst ourselves, when someone rounded on me and asked what I thought of the reading of the Holy Scriptures, when I had hitherto studied only philosophy. I replied that concentration on such reading was most beneficial for the salvation of the soul, but that I found it most surprising that for educated men the writings or glosses of the Fathers themselves were not sufficient for interpreting their commentaries without further instruction. There was general laughter, and I was asked by many of those present if I could or would tackle this myself. I said I was ready to try if they wished. Still laughing, they shouted 'Right, that's settled! Take some commentary on a little-known text and we'll test what you say.' Then they all agreed on an extremely obscure prophecy of Ezekiel. I took the commentary and promptly invited them all to hear my interpretation the very next day. They then pressed unwanted advice on me, telling me not to hurry over something so important but to remember my inexperience and give longer thought to working out and confirming my exposition. I replied indignantly that it was not my custom to benefit by practice, but I relied on my own intelligence, and either they must come to my lecture at the time of my choosing or I should abandon it altogether.
>
> At my first lecture there were certainly not many people present, for everyone thought it absurd that I could attempt this so soon, when up to now I had made no study at all of the Scriptures. But all those who came approved, so that they commended the lecture warmly, and urged me to comment on the text on the same lines as my lecture. The news brought people who had missed my first lecture flocking to the second and third ones, all alike most eager to make copies of the glosses which I had begun with on the first day.[34]

[34] *Historia Calamitatum*, 64f.

Clearly Abelard had found in dialectic a useful and legitimate key but, as one writer describes it, dialectic 'had the same corrosive effect upon true religion and sound learning that psychology has in our day. It was essentially a study of form rather than of content, and so it was a playground of critical minds, concerned with every aspect of intellectual inquiry while sitting lightly to the subject-matter of any of them.'[35]

Against the success of such an approach to the Scriptures, the Cistercians were to develop the monastic tradition of *lectio divina*, making the prayerful pondering of the Bible the centre of their lives; and in order to support the suggestion of a connection between Abelard's attitude to the exposition of Scripture and his castration, it is necessary to discuss that tradition in the communities of monks that nurtured Bernard and, eventually, Abelard, for the thesis depends on the view of the Bible embodied in it.

The attitude of the monk to *lectio divina* is that of a man who has come to himself and knows at last that he is in a far country. He knows, that is, that he is a sinner, alienated from God and habituated to the pigsty of his own sins. But now he *remembers* and, in reading the Scriptures, he rises and begins the long return. Every word draws him nearer because every word is the Word of his Father to whom he will say, when he gets near enough, 'Father, I have sinned against heaven, and in thy sight, and am no more worthy to be called thy son.' (Luke 15:21). But one of the difficulties of the way back is that the language in which the Father speaks has been forgotten. And so the monk, in reading the Word of God, *listens* as though to a foreign tongue in which he is a beginner. He is anxious to get it right, as the servant of a great king is anxious to interpret his lord's commands correctly, or as the lover is anxious to understand the desires of the beloved. But, alas, the king talks in riddles and the beloved whispers inaudibly—or so it seems to the monk, for he is still in the land of unlikeness. Sometimes, perhaps even often, the Word reveals its

35 A. Victor Murray, *Abelard & St Bernard* (Manchester University Press, 1967), 9.

meaning to him and then he is filled with a peculiar joy. But it is a joy always tempered by penitence for he knows that in respect of the Word he has squandered his inheritance and lost his rights and that everything he gains henceforth is pure gift. In any case, his primary purpose in pondering the Scriptures is not for the sake of enlightenment—which might do no more for him than keep him comfortable among the pigs—but for conversion of life. And so St Benedict writes at the beginning of his *Rule:*

> Up with us then at last, for the Scripture arouseth us, saying: *Now is the hour for us to rise from sleep.* Let us open our eyes to the divine light, and let us hear with attentive ears the warning that the divine voice crieth daily to us: *Today if ye will hear his voice, harden not your hearts ...* For the Apostle saith: *Knowest thou not that the patience of God inviteth to repentance?* While the merciful Lord saith: *I will not the death of a sinner, but that he be converted and live.*[36]

Such is the disposition of the monk towards the Scriptures, and the results of it are crucial. For not only is it that he listens attentively to the Word as to a strange, half-understood, half-heard, longed-for language, but that in so doing he *receives* the Word into his soul as seed into the womb or, as in the parable of the sower, 'into the good ground is he that heareth the word, and understandeth it; which also beareth fruit, and bringeth forth, some an hundredfold, some sixty, some thirty' (Matt. 13:23). And the seed is Christ who is thus forever being conceived and growing in the heart until, transformed by his indwelling presence, the monk can say with St Paul: 'I live; yet not I, but Christ liveth in me' (Gal. 2:20).[37]

Now if the monk represents someone in fruitful union with the Word of God, Abelard, I suggest, represents someone in a barren re-

---

[36] Justin McCann OSB, ed. and trans., *The Rule of St Benedict in Latin and English* (Newman Press, 1952), 7 and 11.

[37] See Jean Leclercq, *The Love of Learning and the Desire for God: A Study of Monastic Culture* (Fordham University Press, 1961), for the monk's attitude to *lectio* and *meditatio.*

lationship to it. Barren because he was unable to surrender himself to it and so permit it to penetrate into the silent depths of his being where it could have taken root and grown *within* him. For the principal characteristic we need to note about Abelard is that although he was immensely pious—sometimes movingly so—religion for him remained external. He embodied, as we have seen, that new drive to bring the external world under control, and if control is the aim, the subject of it must be kept under control and not allowed to take it. Hence his unceasingly discursive temperament, incapable of pausing to question itself, resisted every exercise by which Christ might have entered and been quickened in his soul. Consequently his theology reflected this failure and, in turn, his life reflected and was ruined by his theology. For Christ saves from within, and except he be within no amount of Christ without can save us. So, when Bernard came to write his 'Treatise against Abelard' he seized vigorously on this weakness: 'Did Jesus, then, teach righteousness and not *bestow* it? Did he show charity and not *infuse* it, and did he so return to his heaven?'[38]

> What profits it [Bernard goes on] that Jesus should instruct us if he did not first restore us by his grace? Or are we in vain instructed if the body of sin is not first destroyed in us, that we should no more serve sin? If all the benefit that we derive from Christ consists in the exhibition of his virtues, it follows that Adam must be said to harm us only by the exhibition of sin. But in truth the medicine given was proportioned to the disease. *For as in Adam all die, even so in Christ shall all be made alive.* As is the one so is the other. If the life which Christ gives is nothing else but his instruction, the death which Adam gave is in like manner only his instruction; so that the one by his example leads men to sin, the other by his example and his word leads them to a holy life and to love him. But if we ... confess that by generation and not by example was the sin of Adam imparted to us, and by sin death, let us confess that it is necessary for righteousness to be restored to us by Christ, not by instruction *but by*

[38] 'Treatise against Abelard' (Letter 190), *Life and Works of Saint Bernard,* trans. and ed. S. J. Eales (J. Hodges, 1896), vol. II, 583.

> *regeneration* ... And if this be so, how can Peter [Abelard] say that the only purpose and cause of the Incarnation was that he might enlighten the world by the light of his wisdom and inflame it with love of him? Where, then, is redemption? There come from Christ, he says, merely illumination and enkindling to love. Whence come redemption and liberation?[39]

'Whence', for Abelard, indeed, since, as Bernard rightly shows in this passage, he believed only in an external Christ—with what results in his life let us briefly examine.

'Be careful what you wish for, for you shall surely have it'—warns an old proverb. Abelard had been driven step by step through a particular, and particularly compelling, situation to want the final effecting in his body of that which was already a reality in his soul. But the fulfilment of an unrecognized wish inevitably evokes a reaction against it. Abelard's first reaction to the disaster—or, rather, his second, because his first reaction to every disaster always concerned his reputation, his perennial preoccupation—was that the justice of God had struck him in the part of the body with which he had sinned; while chief among many other humiliating reflections he was 'also appalled to remember that according to the cruel letter of the Law, a eunuch is such an abomination to the Lord that men made eunuchs by the amputation or mutilation of their members are forbidden to enter a church ...'.[40] But later his satisfaction at being thus permanently delivered from the 'contagion of carnal impurity'[41] emerged in the view that he had been uniquely singled out, not for God's justice but for his mercy:

> How mercifully did he want me to suffer so much only in that member, the privation of which would also further the salvation of my soul without defiling my body nor preventing any performance

[39] *Life and Works of Saint Bernard*, II, 583.

[40] *Historia Calamitatum*, 76.

[41] Letter 4, Radice, *Letters of Abelard and Héloïse*, 148.

> of my duties! ... So when divine grace cleansed rather than deprived me of those vile members which from their practice of utmost indecency are called 'the parts of shame' and have no proper name of their own, what else did it do but remove a foul imperfection in order to preserve purity?[42]

He then goes on to show that he is superior to Origen because he was, blameless of the deed[43] and more favoured than St Paul who besought the Lord to rid him of this 'thorn in the flesh' (2 Cor. 12:7–8), but was not heard.

> In my case, through God's compassion, it was done by another's hand. I do not incur blame, I escape it. I deserve death and gain life. I am called but hold back; I persist in crime and am pardoned against my will. The Apostle prays and is not heard, he persists in prayer and is not answered. Truly the Lord takes thought for me. I will go then and declare how much the Lord has done for my soul.[44]

All this, and much else besides, gives an overwhelming impression that Abelard is missing the point. He rightly feels his case to be unique but his moralizings obscure the cause. For in him we can see

---

[42] Letter 4, Radice, *Letters of Abelard and Héloïse*, 148.

[43] In fact, Eusebius's story of Origen's self-mutilation is now regarded sceptically by some scholars. See Henry Chadwick, *Early Christian Thought and the Classical Tradition* (Oxford University Press, 1984), 67f. and notes. The evidence from Origen is against it. In his *Commentary on Matthew* (XV.1–5) he discusses the passage about eunuchs and is concerned that it should not be taken literally. The only knife Origen will tolerate is the spiritual knife, namely, the Word: 'Those who receive the "living and active Word, sharper than any two-edged sword", as the apostle says, and cuts off his concupiscence, not touching his body, and makes himself thus, not because, of the praise of men, or fear of them, but only because of the hope of the heavenly kingdom—these are they who have made themselves eunuchs for the sake of the kingdom of God.' But Abelard did not, apparently, read Greek, and the Latin translation of the *Commentary on Matthew* is selective and does not include Origen's discussion on self-emasculation. (I am indebted to Revd Prof. Andrew Louth for the information in this note.)

[44] Letter 4, Radice, *Letters of Abelard and Héloïse*, 149.

the truth that the cause of lust becoming uncontrollable in direct opposition to the will is to be found not in lust itself but in the activity of pride, in particular in that aspect called presumption—Abelard's chief characteristic.

Héloïse, on the other hand, although inclined to play Echo to Abelard's Narcissus, does not moralize about their relationship. Jean Leclercq points out that the contrast between them

> appears even in the vocabulary applied to the same experiences: when Héloïse speaks of 'desires', 'delights', 'sensuous pleasures' as being realities which were and still are 'sweet' and 'agreeable', Abelard mentions only 'turpitudes', 'impurities', 'fornications', and 'abominations'.[45]

Héloïse does not reflect Abelard's censorious attitude because she was in love with him—and lust is always subject to love. Consequently it remained in her as an ever-present power, giving energy both to her spiritual development and to her practical abilities. At the same time her constant and agonizing awareness of it kept her humble ('I do not seek a crown of victory; it is sufficient for me to avoid danger ...'[46]) and free from the illusion of loving God for himself alone—an illusion with which those who enter the religious state of their own free choice are, in the nature of the case, liable to be afflicted.[47] This is not to say that Héloïse was all white and Abelard all black. They were a finely matched pair. One could even make a case for Abelard being more in love with Héloïse than she

45 Jean Leclercq OSB, 'Modern Psychology and the Interpretation of Medieval Texts', *Speculum,* 48/3 (July 1973), 484. But see also Southern's essay, easily the best account: 'The Letters of Abelard and Héloïse', in *Medieval Humanism.*

46 Letter 3, Radice, *Letters of Abelard and Héloïse,* 135.

47 One should mention—and a footnote seems an appropriate place—that Héloïse and Abelard had a son called, by Héloïse, Astrolabe. The author's awareness of the authenticity discussions should also be noted. But if the psychological authenticity of the letters between Héloïse and Abelard is understood, further discussion can only seem a waste of time.

with him. She was, I think, largely sustained in her tragedy by being a terrific role-player and by the incomparable advantage of being devoid of humour. Indeed, had there been a flicker of humour in her personality Abelard would undoubtedly have dropped her like a hot brick in the first round and we would never have heard of her. The immense seriousness with which she recognized it was essential to take him must have had its counterpart in her attitude towards herself. Abelard, indeed, understood that, in comparison with himself, Héloïse had the better part since 'for the one who must always strive there is also a crown … But no crown is waiting for me because no cause of striving remains'.[48] While earlier in the same letter he exclaims to the still-young but already-revered abbess:

> How great an interest the talent of your own wisdom pays daily to the Lord in the many spiritual daughters you have borne for him, while I remain totally barren and labour in vain amongst the sons of perdition![49]

In spite of what he writes, he is clearly thinking primarily of himself when he sums up his feelings about the purpose of his castration:

> See, then, how greatly the Lord was concerned for us, as if he were reserving us for some great ends, and was indignant or grieved because our knowledge of letters, the talents which he had entrusted to us, were not being used to glorify his name …[50]

[48] Letter 4, Radice, *Letters of Abelard and Héloïse*, 154.
[49] Letter 4, Radice, *Letters of Abelard and Héloïse*, 150.
[50] Letter 4, Radice, *Letters of Abelard and Héloïse*, 149.

The Thinker

Abelard, being now about forty years of age, began at once those writings and lectures that were to occupy him for the next twenty years of his life until the final disaster of excommunication at Sens. Having entered the abbey of Saint-Denis he had scarcely, he tells us, recovered from his wound before

> the clerks came thronging round to pester the abbot and myself with repeated demands that I should now for the love of God continue the studies which hitherto I had pursued only in desire for wealth and fame …

And so,

> … I first applied myself to lecturing on the basis of our faith by analogy with human reason, and composed a theological treatise 'On the Unity and Trinity of God' for the use of my students who were asking for human and logical reasons on this subject, and demanded something intelligible rather than mere words. In fact they said that words were useless if the intelligence could not follow them, that nothing could be believed unless it was first understood, and that it was absurd for anyone to preach to others what neither he nor those he taught could grasp with the understanding: the Lord himself criticised such 'blind guides of blind men.' After the treatise had been seen and read by many people I began to please everyone, as it seemed to answer all questions alike on this subject. It was generally agreed that the questions were peculiarly difficult and the importance of the problem was matched by the subtlety of my solution.[51]

However, this treatise, which solved—according to human and logical reasons, and to the satisfaction of young students—the

[51] *Historia Calamitatum*, 78.

problems of the Trinity, did not, after all, please everyone and, in 1121, two years after his mutilation, it was condemned at the Council of Soissons.

That this Council was as brutish in its way as Fulbert's revenge had been may be allowed from Abelard's account. The proceedings, indeed, gave him ample opportunity for drawing his favourite comparison—that between himself and Christ. But if the situation bore marks of similarity they were confined to the situation and did not extend to Abelard's own behaviour which signally failed to follow that example he held to be the means of grace. For whereas when Jesus 'was accused of the chief priests and elders, he answered nothing' (Matt. 27:12), Abelard played into his enemies hands by being all too eager to justify himself, pouring forth a torrent of explanations, until silenced, which only succeeded in further confusing the issue and hardening opinion against him:

> My former betrayal seemed small in comparison with the wrongs I now had to endure, and I wept much more for the injury done to my reputation than for the damage to my body, for that I had brought upon myself through my own fault, but this open violence had come upon me only because of the purity of *my* intentions and love of our Faith which had compelled me to write.[52]

Happily the damage to his reputation was soon repaired and he was able to escape from the goodness and kindness of the abbot and monks of St Medard, where he had been confined after the condemnation, back to his own monastery which, being 'completely worldly and depraved',[53] provided an ambience conducive to his sense of moral superiority—now added to his sense of intellectual superiority.

Needless to say he did not last at Saint-Denis. While reading Bede he discovered that their patron was not to be identified with the Dionysius the Areopagite of Acts 17:34, a discovery he pointed out to

[52] *Historia Calamitatum*, 85.

[53] *Historia Calamitatum*, 77.

some of the brethren 'by way of a joke'.[54] No one laughed, however, and he was compelled to flee from their lack of humour on the subject. In due course—his one piece of fortune in the midst of all his calamities—he was able to take possession of a piece of land in a lonely spot under the jurisdiction of the Bishop of Troyes.

At first he dedicated this place to the Trinity but re-named it, very unusually, the Paraclete on account of the comfort in his despair he had found there. His sensitivity to criticism obliged him to defend this name at length,[55] and with his usual overtones of self-pity, but it is here we get a glimpse for the first time in the *Historia* of a serious and independent thinker. It is here also, in his life at the Paraclete, that Abelard's attraction for the times is most clearly demonstrated; for it is one thing to flock to a teacher in the town where one already is, but quite another to go after him into the country, as Abelard so vividly describes:

> No sooner was this known than the students began to gather there from all parts, hurrying from cities and towns to inhabit the wilderness, leaving large mansions to build themselves little huts, eating wild herbs and coarse bread instead of delicate food, spreading reeds and straw in place of soft beds and using banks of turf for tables.[56]

Abelard spent about three years in this place, while his pupils provided

> all I needed, unasked, food, clothing, work on the land as well as building expenses ... As my oratory could not hold even a modest

---

[54] *Historia Calamitatum*, 26. Bede wrote that Dionysius was Bishop of Corinth, and not of Athens, as was believed. Athens was far more important than Corinth, and relocating him was a significant downgrade in status, with resulting dishonour brought on the convent of St-Denis, no less than only the French royal family, for whom St Denis was their patron saint. Abelard thought it funny, but the repercussions for the acceptance of Bede in France were enormous, while Abelard's defence of Bede led to him being branded an enemy of the monastery. See Dario Lisiero, *Abelard and Heloise. Between the Lines* (Lulu.com, 2012), 53–4.

[55] *Historia Calamitatum*, 91.

[56] *Historia Calamitatum*, 88.

> proportion of their numbers, they were obliged to enlarge it, and improved it by building in wood and stone.[57]

Inevitably all this aroused the envy *(invidia,* a word which recurs throughout the *Historia Calamitatum,* being, of course, the same as that used in the Vulgate of the enemies of Christ) of his rivals and they complained that 'all the world has gone after him' (John 12:19). 'We have gained nothing by persecuting him,' they said, 'only increased his fame. We meant to extinguish the light of his name but all we have done is to make it shine still brighter.'[58]

This was clearly an impressive period, but to sustain it would have required the kind of virtues Abelard had never developed—summed up for the monk in the one word: stability. And so, full of fears for the persecutions he thought were being directed against him ('God is my witness that I never heard that an assembly of ecclesiastics had met without thinking this was convened to condemn me.'[59]), combined with his apparent inability to control his disorderly students,[60] he accepted the abbacy of Saint-Gildas de Rhuys, some 360 miles away in a wild spot on the west coast of Brittany. Thus he exchanged a difficult but fruitful situation for an impossible and barren one; disorderly but devoted students for disorderly and murderous monks.

However, the ill wind which blew Abelard to Brittany enabled him two years later in 1128 to house Héloïse, and those of her nuns who remained with her, at the Paraclete when Suger, now abbot of Saint-Denis, claimed the convent at Argenteuil as the property of that monastery. The contact—the first for ten years between Abelard and Héloïse—during these negotiations seems to have been entirely impersonal, it never occurring to Abelard that Héloïse's feelings had not

---

57 *Historia Calamitatum,* 46. In fact his students rebelled, as described by Hilary of Orléans. See Michael T. Clanchy, *Abelard: A Medieval Life* (Blackwell, 1999), 240–1.

58 *Historia Calamitatum,* 90.

59 *Historia Calamitatum,* 93.

60 *Historia Calamitatum,* 94, n. 1.

been stifled with his own which, if one were able to gauge such things, would surely provide an all-time record of the effect of self-pity on the imagination. But a few years later in 1132, while still at St Gildas, Abelard wrote the *Historia* and a copy came into Héloïse's hands. In consequence she took up her pen and re-opened the relationship in a manner calculated to pierce even Abelard's self-absorption. Having succeeded in the course of two extremely personal letters in gaining his full attention—or, at least, very much more of it than he normally spared from himself—she held it, and the efforts she put him to on behalf of herself and her community are the best, in the sense of being the least egotistical and most disinterested, he ever made. At her request he poured out hymns and sermons and advice in abundance, and his Rule for the Paraclete has some fine passages in it and shows an intimate knowledge of monastic life, even if the tedious tenor of its style would hardly inspire anyone to live it.

After Héloïse's installation as abbess of the Paraclete, Bernard went there to preach, the Paraclete being not far from Clairvaux. Héloïse told Abelard that Bernard was more like an angel than a man but reported privately that Bernard had criticized their use of Matthew's version of the Lord's Prayer instead of, as was then customary, the Lucan version.[61] Abelard rose to this criticism with his usual heat and wrote Bernard a letter in which he argued an excellent case in favour of the Matthean version concluding with: 'Whoever he be let him notice that use is not to be preferred to reason nor custom to truth',[62] a saying Abelard often repeated and which conveys briefly both the appeal and the limitation of his thought.

There is no further record of direct contact between Abelard and Bernard until 1138 when William of St Thierry aroused Bernard with an anguished letter written as a result of reading Abelard's

[61] Letter from Abelard to the abbot of Clairvaux in the 1130s. See Constant J. Mews, *The Lost Love Letters of Heloise and Abelard: Perceptions of Dialogue in Twelfth-Century France, with a translsation by Neville Chiavaroli and Constant J. Mews* (2nd edn Palgrave Macmillan, 2008), 159.

[62] Quoted in Murray, *Abelard & St Bernard*, 35.

Introductio ad theologiam and *Theologia christiana* which a novice had brought with him to William's monastery at Signy. Abelard, meanwhile, had gained release from his abbey of St Gildas but with the right to retain the rank of abbot, and in these last few years, through a mixture of stretches of teaching in Paris combined with stretches of disappearance (which in a more esoteric character would lend themselves to speculations), had acquired immense prestige. So William writes: 'Fear lest we offend a man of standing drives from our hearts the fear of offending God!'[63]—which, of course, effectively engaged Bernard in battle.

After some preliminary and apparently amicable skirmishes between Bernard and Abelard it became clear that Abelard had no intention of modifying his views in accordance with Bernard's requirements. Bernard then preached against Abelard and Abelard retaliated by challenging Bernard to a confrontation, not doubting that in debate he could confound the Abbot of Clairvaux. It seems that Bernard also expected to be confounded, and the view generally held at the time of writing is that Bernard's reluctance to meet Abelard in open debate was due to his sense of being out of his depth in the face of Abelard's greater dialectical skill. But if a dog challenges an elephant to a swimming contest in a stretch of water which at no point rises higher than the elephant's knees, can the elephant be said to be out of his depth because he cannot swim in it? And this analogy precisely conveys the frustration the intuitive person feels in relation to the logical person, and would alone account for Bernard's excitement—although in a longer study it would be interesting to explore other possibilities.

Abelard chose a great public occasion to meet Bernard—a solemn exposition of relics at Sens in the presence of the King of France

---

[63] The text of this letter is given almost in full in Jean-Marie Déchanet's valuable book, *William of St Thierry*, Cistercian Studies 10 (Cistercian Publications, 1972), 55. Approaching Abelard through William of St Thierry is far more instructive than approaching him through Bernard, and I regret that lack of space prevented me pursuing that line here.

and most of the bishops—and arrived for it surrounded by disciples, the principal one at this time being Arnald of Brescia. Arnald, under the guise of extreme austerity of life, was a particularly nasty rabble-rouser who had lately been expelled from his own country but was destined to return there and, after many years of successful terrorism in Rome, to be hanged. That Abelard should have been yoked to a man whose career and character were alike repellent is significant and suggests something of that interior disintegration which was about to be revealed.

Bernard brought nineteen charges against Abelard,[64] a large number of which Abelard could easily have sported with for as long as anyone remained interested. Instead he was suddenly speechless in that great assembly, like the man who 'had not on a wedding garment' (Matt. 22:11). The intellectual structure he had built up was unexpectedly shown to be hollow as it collapsed in the face of Bernard's fullness of heart and mind. Spiritual sterility challenged spiritual fecundity, and he was ashamed because he had no children to speak with his enemies in the gate.[65]

And so Abelard, unable to utter a word in his own defence, was condemned. For a brief account of the last lap, Knowles cannot be bettered:

> He appealed to Rome, and set out for the threshold of the Apostles, preceded by a bunch of the fiercest and most devastating letters ever written by St Bernard, but was intercepted on the road by Peter the Venerable, abbot of Cluny, who received him with characteristic sympathy, gave him a home in his own great abbey, and advised him to retract what was clearly erroneous or rash in his teaching. Abelard, with what searchings of heart we know not, took the wise

---

[64] For a short and highly comprehensible account of the *capitula* see Edward Little, 'Bernard and Abelard at the Council of Sens, 1140', in *Bernard of Clairvaux, Studies Presented to Dom Jean Leclercq*, ed. by M. Basil Pennington, Cistercian Studies 23 (Cistercian Publications, 1973), 55–71. For a longer study see Murray, *Abelard & St Bernard*.

[65] Cf. Ps. 127.

if unexpected decision to follow this advice, and at a meeting with St Bernard complete harmony was established in personal relations, though Abelard's retractation stopped at the minimum possible, while in a final apologia he gave the abbot of Clairvaux as good as he had received, Back at Cluny, well over sixty and an invalid, he was still active as a writer. He had been condemned by the pope, but Peter, furnished with his retractation, obtained permission for him to remain undisturbed at Cluny. His last year was a surprising and moving contrast to his earlier life; he lived in submission and simplicity till April 1142, when he died in peace in a priory of Cluny at Chalon-sur-Saone. It was then that Peter the Venerable wrote to Héloïse that most remarkable letter in which, besides expressing his admiration for herself and Abelard, he refers to their old association and anticipates their reunion beyond the tomb, 'where, beyond these voices, there is peace'.[66]

[66] Knowles, *Evolution of Medieval Thought*, 120.

Abelard's Writings

At the time of writing the only works of Abelard's available in English are his *Ethics,* the *Historia Calamitatum* and the correspondence with Héloïse. But translators are doubtless working on the rest and it will not be too long, one supposes, before there is a single publication entitled 'The Complete Works of Peter Abelard'.[67] It will include less than a dozen works, most of them relatively short treatises, the more important being *De unitate et trinitate divina,* the work condemned at Soissons; and the three from which the nineteen *capitula* were taken and condemned at Sens: *Introductio ad theologiam, Theologia christiana,* and *Epitome theologia christiana.* It will also include the collection of contradictory sayings from Scripture and the Fathers, *Sic et Non;* and a number of slighter treatises such as the *Dialogue between the Christian, the Philosopher and the Jew* and the *Commentary on Romans,* as well as those works in translation already mentioned.

Of Abelard's theological treatises, which landed him in so much trouble, Southern says the earliest version, condemned at Soissons, 'is the sharpest and best and shows what he really thought'.[68] Thereafter he amended and qualified and tried, with his usual desire to have things both ways: to express his opinions in forms at once orthodox and alarming. That is, he hoped to upset orthodox opinion but without giving orthodox opinion any grounds for upsetting him in return. As these tactics have been brought to a point of refinement among professional theologians in our day it is hard for us to share

[67] At the time of this new edition there remains no 'complete works' of Abelard, although there are collections of the letters and of his philosophical and ethical writings. Ed.

[68] Southern, Lectures on 'Abelard, his Friends and his Enemies'.

the excitement Abelard aroused in his day for, in comparison with modern theologians, he looks like a veritable beginner at the business—which, of course, historically, is exactly what he was.

Of his other works, *Sic et Non* seems to have generated the most friction. 'Even now', Southern says, 'there is something shocking about flinging down so large a body of contradictions without any attempt to reconcile them.'[69] Jean-Marie Déchanet on the other hand—and he is not the only one—calls it 'that great book'[70] which, however, seems to be a judgement urged rather by the current compulsion to over-rate Abelard than by any intrinsic merit in the work. This compulsion is shown most clearly by David Luscombe at the end of his otherwise excellent introduction to the *Ethics*, which is called—or rather miscalled, since there is nothing in it likely to contribute to that end–*Know Thyself*. 'The text itself', writes Luscombe, 'is bracing and exciting in its argumentation [and] also somewhat spicy, for Abelard had a vivid sexual imagination.'[71] (No doubt this is intended to encourage the reader to endure the tediousness of reading Abelard himself.) 'Moreover,' continues Luscombe (in case it does not),

> Abelard did not mince words when expressing his dissatisfaction with the quality of the prelates of his own day or with the contemporary nobility. In this way his work leads us back from the task of speculation and of introspection to the reappraisal of the real world of practical and social endeavour.

Since *Know Thyself* seems to consist of series of barren speculations on unlikely contingencies ('For example,' writes Abelard, 'if someone compels a Religious who is bound in chains to lie between women and if he is brought to pleasure, not to consent, by the softness of the bed and through contact with the women, who may presume … ' and so on) one can only ask: to which 'real world' does Professor Luscombe refer?

---

69 Southern, Lectures on 'Abelard, his Friends and his Enemies'.

70 Déchanet, *William of St Thierry*, 4.

71 David E. Luscombe, ed. and trans., *Peter Abelard's Ethics: An edition with introduction, English translation and notes* (Clarendon Press, 1971), xxxvii.

It is possible that if one were to read all of Abelard's works he would emerge in a light more commensurate with the praise he is at present receiving. But it is more likely that when his entire output can be seen whole it will become impossible to continue inflating his reputation and that he will then subside into a suitable place among the world's tenth-rate thinkers. Leaving aside his role in the development of Scholasticism has he, then, any real importance? In the Letters of Direction to Héloïse, Abelard quotes a beautiful passage from Origen which sums up his own view of his role:

> Those wells which the Philistines had filled with earth are surely men who close their spiritual understanding, so that they neither drink themselves nor allow others to drink. Hear the word of the Lord: 'Alas for you lawyers and Pharisees! You have taken away the key of knowledge; you did not go in yourselves, and did not permit those who wished to enter.' But let us never cease from digging wells of living water, and by discussing new things as well as old, let us make ourselves like the teacher of the law in the Gospel of whom the Lord said that he could 'produce from his store both old and new.' Let us return to Isaac and dig with him wells of living water, even if the Philistines obstruct us; even if they use violence, let us carry on with our well-digging, so that to us too it may be said: 'Drink water from your own cisterns and your own wells.' And let us dig until our wells overflow with water in our courtyards, so that our knowledge of the Scriptures is not only sufficient for ourselves, but we can teach others and show them how to drink.[72]

The disparity between Origen and Abelard is as great as it could be (although Abelard desired to be Origen's peer), and yet there is a sense in which Abelard was right in feeling that his function was to oppose the forces of philistinism. The Philistines provide recurring occasions of conflict in the Church and have to be resisted in every generation. So it is not the necessity of digging afresh the wells of living water or of issuing forth against Goliath which is in question but the character of the person who takes upon themselves these tasks.

---

[72] Radice, *Letters of Abelard and Héloïse*, 267.

This brings us to a consideration of Abelard's one work, the *Historia Calamitatum*, which, for genuine interest, is a brilliant exception to all the rest.

Experiments in autobiography were beginning to be made at this time, a fact which in itself indicates a radically altered attention, but Abelard's was unique and marked a new development in introspection. Its original title was, *Abaelardi ad amicum suum consolatoria* ('Abelard's letter of consolation to his friend'), and although this may have been a conventional device, given Abelard's desire to improve upon every situation, it is quite likely that he used the misfortunes of an actual friend as a springboard for recounting his own. In any event, it is written in a style—although in accordance with the conventions of the times—more likely to arouse wrath than assuage grief: 'In comparison with my trials you will see that your own are nothing, or only slight, and will find them easier to bear.'[73] The recipient, if he existed, doubtless must have felt on reading it that a letter of consolation from Abelard ranked fairly high in comparison with Abelard's trials.

The account, which takes Abelard up to his early fifties when, it appears, he was still Abbot of St Gildas, is written in a vivid, compressed style which, together with its selectivity—it amounts to less than fifty pages in translation—makes every line contributory to the total effect. The immediate aim seems to be a desire to forestall further criticism by supplying abundant material for it and then getting in first. The ultimate aim is more mysterious. For there is a compelling quality about the *Historia Calamitatum* which raises it to a level above ordinary interpretation and justifies attempts to see in it something of universal significance. This compelling quality is due, I believe, to it being an inspired work and Abelard its unconscious but wholly appropriate vehicle. Abelard is compelled to reveal, for 'those who have ears to hear' (Matt. 11:15), the whole psychology of spiritual sterility. That, at any rate, is my view. But it is worth noting a more sympathetic one. Mary McLaughlin has written:

---

[73] *Historia Calamitatum*, 57.

Sharing with Luther and Kierkegaard, among others, a passion for describing and expressing his sufferings, he seems to belong with them to the company of those reformers and innovators whose personal sufferings and struggles have a public significance, who are destined not only to participate actively in, but to endure and articulate in their extreme forms, certain crucial experiences and transformations of their times. Impelled, whether consciously or not, to take on the most arduous tasks of their societies, such men are commonly possessed by a sense of vocation or mission that is a major source of their peculiarly symbiotic relationships with the larger movements of their times. In Abelard's case, as in others of this kind, the sense of a special calling appears to have developed early, and it was to become central to his later efforts at self-definition.[74]

This is magnificently expressed and captures a vital truth about Abelard. In fact, on looking into it, there is much to disagree with. Abelard was not, it is now seen, a reformer nor an innovator. He was a popularizer of rising trends. Southern calls him a 'brilliant meteoric irritant in a period of disarray in medieval thought before the consolidation of the mid-twelfth century'.[75] And Reginald Lane Poole, in a rare moment of sober estimate, confines Abelard to the status of being 'first and foremost a critic' and goes on:

The love of opposition was his normal stimulus to production; and the fact that the object of his attack held one view led him inevitably to emphasize the contrary.[76]

Likewise it is difficult to share Mary McLaughlin's grand view (described above) of the sufferings of a man in whom feeling was confined to self-pity. Nevertheless it is true that his personal sufferings had a public significance and that he had to endure and articulate certain crucial experiences which expressed the transformations of

74 Mary McLaughlin, 'Abelard as Autobiographer: The Motives and Meaning of his *Story of Calamities*', *Speculum*, 42/3 (1967), 463–88.

75 Southern, Lectures on 'Abelard, his Friends and his Enemies'.

76 Reginald Lane Poole, *Illustrations of the History of Medieval Thought and Learning* (Dover Publications, 1960), 140, first published in 1884.

the times. But that was because, in taking on the arduous tasks of his society, he showed himself to be not so much an Isaac or a David as another Goliath, arrogant and certain of his invincibility, whose presumption ('Ye have heard that it hath been said by them of old time ... But *I* say ...' was Abelard's oft-repeated line) rendered him impotent in relation to life, and finally drew out a true David against him. That the true David is generally regarded nowadays as the leader of the Philistines is itself a philistine verdict and belongs peculiarly to that combination of romanticism and rationalism which, as I noted at the beginning, emerged in the nineteenth century. It produced a type of thinker for whom Abelard provided, and continues to provide, a welcome relief from the implications of real thought—that is, of thought which has its roots in the heart.

As Far as Thought Can Reach

This is the title of the last part of Shaw's play *Back to Methuselah* and a critic, using it to comment on Shaw himself, wrote: 'It is not very far; for thought is the formulation of feeling, and where feeling has been stifled thought has little to work on.'[77] That was precisely Abelard's case. The comment could also be applied to Bertrand Russell—to whom Southern likens Abelard—and both Shaw and Russell are typical of that climate of thought which rescued Abelard from the obscurity into which he had fallen after his death (being remembered through the centuries chiefly for the drama with Héloïse) and which rapturously hailed him as a herald of enlightenment and the first apostle of free thought. Abelard had to wait for recognition until an era that was compatible with his character and, although the view of him as a free thinker broke down under the first dispassionate examination of him, we are still, psychologically, in the same era. What, then, does that suggest to us about his character and our era?

In the chapter called 'The Emergence of Modern Man' we saw the change in direction of a person's attention from God to oneself which occurred on entering the millennium, and the division, after Anselm, between spiritual growth—represented by Bernard—and technological and intellectual growth—represented by Abelard—and their independent development. This division between spiritual and intellectual growth is peculiar to Latin Christendom. It did not occur in Greek Christendom, or rather, one should say, it did not occur in the same way. The division in Greek Christendom has been—far more intensely than in the West—between the 'Jewish' and the 'Greek' psychologies. But whereas in the West the Greek side has tended to

[77] Hugh Kingsmill [Lunn], *The Progress of a Biographer* (Methuen, 1949), 48.

degenerate into a barren intellectualism, in the East spiritual power has been maintained in both camps. It is significant that the final schism between Latin and Greek Christendom actually took place in those years (the date usually given is 1054) when in the West spirituality and theology began to fall apart.

It is, furthermore, significant that Abelard was the first to use this word 'theology' in the sense now current in all European countries, that is, in the sense of being separate from spirituality.[78] But this separation did not, as it were, come to full harvest until the nineteenth century, when the long chain of cause and effect culminated in a final shift. Whereas the 'triumph of Anselm's analytical introspective method' had been to discover God on looking into himself, people now discovered themselves on looking inwards, and no longer as 'bearing within themselves a feeble image of the ineffable prototype', in Gregory of Sinai's words, but as being—via the apes—the peak of the evolutionary process. Since then we have been falling apart at a tremendous pace until it is no longer possible to say what the divisions are. In 1976 Anthony Hanson opened an article in *The Times* with the words: 'Any day now I expect one of my students will hand in an essay beginning: "Many mathematicians feel that two and two make four".'[79] He went on to say that the word 'feels' is now being used to do duty for 'believes', 'holds', 'is convinced', 'claims'—almost 'knows'. Reason, apparently, is a bourgeois illusion, and Nietzsche, Marx, and Freud between them have rendered appeal to it in vain.

So the problem is no longer that of the exaltation of reason divorced from feeling but of the fragmentation and confusion of both divorced from their source of unity. And this was what Bernard foresaw, as Pieper says in his book, *Scholasticism:*

> Bernard's passionate and truly 'philosophical' interest was entirely directed toward full 'realization,' toward existential Wholeness,

[78] See Knowles, *Evolution of Medieval Thought*, 126.

[79] Anthony Hanson, 'The Struggle for the Vindication of Reason', *The Times*, 8 May 1976.

> which is to say 'salvation'. And he regarded all forms of human expression, his philosophising as well as his theology, as designed to serve that Whole. It was precisely this kind of salvation that Bernard considered to be endangered and undermined by 'dialecticians' of the type of Abelard. The danger which he quite rightly saw dawning in such personalities, and which he fought with all his might, was nothing less than this: that the substance of Truth, by which living man is nourished, would be consumed by an empty formalism of 'correct' thinking consumed and reduced to vanishing point.[80]

If we look at the heirs of Abelard—very much in the ascendance in academic circles—we see that we have arrived at that vanishing point, for the present function of theology seems largely to consist in telling us what it is no longer possible—or 'correct'—to believe. On reading, for instance, Wiles's *The Remaking of Christian Doctrine*,[81] one is left with the impression that the author—as one might expect in this technological age—possesses a magic 'disappearing' aerosol spray (one puff for the Atonement; puff, puff for the Incarnation; puff, puff, puff—and that was the Trinity that was!); while another, equally symptomatic book by an Oxbridge theologian has been described by one critic as '£5.00's worth of hesitation'. Such nervy agnosticism starts back in dismay from the vitality and assurance of Bernard:

> Far be it from us, then, to suppose that the Christian faith has as its boundaries those opinions of the Academicians, whose boast it is they doubt of everything and know nothing. But I for my part walk securely ... and I know I shall not be confounded.[82]

And yet I am bound to say that the effect of reading *The Remaking of Christian Doctrine* was rather to make me concerned about monasticism: 'Of course, this kind of theologizing is wrong, but we have only ourselves to blame for it', I thought, borrowing from the remark

[80] Josef Pieper, *Scholasticism: Personalities and Problems of Medieval Philosophy* (Faber & Faber, 1961), 90.

[81] Maurice Wiles, *The Remaking of Christian Doctrine* (SCM Press, 1974).

[82] 'Treatise against Abelard', *Life and Works of Saint Bernard*, II, 575.

made about Luther by Pope Leo X.[83] I am fully aware that Maurice Wiles represents only a strand in current theology. But, like Abelard, he symbolizes a state of affairs: Abelard at one end and Wiles at the other. And in Wiles one can see that we are again at the end of a road.Which brings me to the one division which can, I think, illuminate our understanding of what has been happening in this 'yesterday' of a thousand years; and that is the division between 'personality' and 'being', which I see as having first manifested itself in permanent contrast in the figures of Bernard and Abelard.

First it is necessary to define the terms. I understand 'personality' in its sense of being derived from *persona*—as once applied to the masks worn by actors—and the sense in which it is used in psychology. Peter Ouspensky, in his book *In Search of the Miraculous,* says of it:

> Personality in man is what is 'not his own'. 'Not his own' means what has come from outside, what he has learned, or reflects, all traces of exterior impressions left in the memory and in the sensations, all words and movements that have been learned, all feelings created by imitation—all this is 'not his own', all this is personality ... A small child has no personality as yet. He is what he really is ... His desires, tastes, likes, dislikes, express his being—such as it is ... Culture creates personality and is at the same time the product and the result of personality. We do not realise that the whole of our life, all we call civilization, all we call science, philosophy, art and politics, is created by people's personality, that is, by what is 'not their own' in them. The element that is 'not his own' differs from what is man's 'own' by the fact that it can be lost, altered, or taken away by artificial means.[84]

[83] Cf. *Exsurge Domine,* papal bull promulgated on 15 June 1520 by Pope Leo X.

[84] Peter D. Ouspensky, *In Search of the Miraculous: Fragments of an Unknown Teaching* (Routledge & Kegan Paul, 1950). This and the following quotation have been extracted from pp. 161–3. Ouspensky, of course, is quoting the teaching of Gurdjieff, and is quoted here in the spirit of 'despoiling the Egyptians' (Ex. 12:36). This is too valuable a jewel to be left behind, even if the setting is 'wrong'.

That which is a person's own is, of course, that 'being' or 'essence' as Ouspensky calls it here:

> In proportion as personality grows, essence manifests itself more and more rarely and more and more feebly, and it often happens that essence stops in its growth at a very early age and grows no further … so that the essence of a grown-up man, even that of a very intellectual and, in the accepted meaning of the word, highly 'educated' man, stops on the level of a child of five or six … Sometimes, though very seldom, and sometimes when it is least expected, essence proves fully grown and fully developed in a man, even in cases of undeveloped personality, and in this case essence unites together everything that is serious and real in a man. But this happens very seldom. As a rule a man's essence is either primitive, savage, and childish, or else simply stupid. The development of essence depends on work on oneself. A very important moment in the work on oneself is when a man begins to distinguish between his personality and his essence … But in order to enable essence to grow up, it is first of all necessary to weaken the constant pressure of personality upon it, because the obstacles to the growth of essence are contained in personality.[85]

This weakening of the constant pressure of personality on essence, or being, so that it may grow, is the function of the monastic life. It provides—or should provide—the means by which there may be created in a person that which is their 'own', is indestructible and cannot be 'lost, altered, or taken away'—'your joy no man taketh from you' (John 16:22). And for this the one thing necessary is that one is not much cumbered about with personality, even in the service of God, for it is as easy to get stuck in personality in relation to God as it is easy to get stuck in it in relation to the world. Monastic discipline, then, is designed to break up the crystallization of personality—whatever form it may have taken. And in the Cistercian tradition, in particular, *lectio divina,* as we have seen, forms a large part of that discipline. For, if the distinction between being and per-

---

[85] Ouspensky, *In Search of the Miraculous,* 161–3.

sonality is understood it can also be understood that all Scripture is written i) from the standpoint of being, ii) by those whose being is united to the Being of God, and iii) for those who desire to be united in their being with the Being of God. And from the standpoint of being, every word of Scripture is true.

All this is not to say that personality is 'bad' and being is 'good'. Personality is necessary; it should, indeed, be the faithful servant of being, while hell, no less than heaven, is inhabited by people of being since only being can survive the shock of death. In what sense, then, does it strike me that the results of personality cut off from being—as manifested today in much theology and biblical criticism—can be charged to the account of monasticism? Writing on Bernard, Knowles has an interesting passage which relates to this point:

> It would be unpardonable, in glancing at the various intellectual currents of the twelfth century, to omit all reference to the dynamic personality of one who, though never precisely a teacher of the schools, was capable, alone of all his contemporaries, of drowning or, if the expression be allowed, of 'jamming' all other voices, and who, on the great web of medieval religious thought and sentiment, changed and formed more patterns than any other man of his century. It is at first sight a paradox that one who, when all is said and done, affected his contemporaries more universally and more profoundly than any of those we have mentioned in the last two chapters, should stand entirely apart from, and should in some ways be positively hostile to, learning of all kinds. In many ways, indeed, the reputation of St Bernard for ferocious mental puritanism is the outcome of a piece of supreme, if unconscious, bluff. Historians and critics have been so occupied in registering their disapproval and framing replies to Bernard's attack on the wordy volubility of philosophers and worldly wisdom that teaches only vanity, or in admiring his profession that his only learning is the cross of Christ, that they have failed to note that they have to deal, not only with a speculative theologian of wide reading and great intellectual power, but with a literary genius of the first order, the greatest master of language in the Middle Ages who, alone of all this age, has a power

equal to that of Demosthenes, of Cicero and of Burke, to carry us with him on the gale of his eloquence ...[86]

As this quotation from Knowles reminds us, although it is right to see a great and deep conflict between Bernard and Abelard—the monasteries and the schools, the claims of contemplation and the demands of the discursive intellect, or, in the terms I have been using, between being and personality—this can be misleading. For while Abelard belongs wholly to one side of the dichotomy, Bernard would dwarf him on either side. The pupil of Saint-Vories towers above his opponents in the schools. Here is a man with a personality developed beyond anything that Abelard, cramped by conceit and self-concern, could show; a man who could beat the schools hollow at their own game *and yet* who threw his genius, his personality, on to the side of being, not on to the side that would have seemed most to foster it. To be detached from personality is a great thing; to be detached from *such* a personality is sanctity of the highest order. No wonder Dante finds Bernard to introduce him to the highest sphere of heaven—the Empyrean:

> ... tale era io mirando la vivace
> carità di colui, che in questo mondo,
> contemplando, gusto di quella pace.
>
> *... such was I, gazing upon the living*
> *love of him who in this world by*
> *contemplation tasted of that peace.*[87]

So, Bernard threw the whole weight of his amazing personality on to the side of being. But was he right? Did he force a wedge between personality and being, thought and feeling, theology and spirituality which without him—notwithstanding Abelard and all he represented—might have retained their true relationship? And did he thus deprive monasticism of its capacity to generate real thought by limiting it to an affective way based wholly on the development

[86] Knowles, *Evolution of Medieval Thought*, 147.

[87] *The Paradiso of Dante Alighieri*, ed. and trans. P. H. Wicksteed, Temple Classics (J. M. Dent, 1899), 381, 'Canto XXXI'.

of being to the exclusion of personality? And did he thereby promote a compartmentalization which on the one hand left being without proper expression and on the other paved the way for that kind of thought which fails to reach far because it issues only from itself and so, inevitably, becomes increasingly disincarnate and narcissistic?

It seems there is a sense in which one must answer 'yes'. For while there are religious in whom personality remains paramount, and academicians in whom being is fully developed, the division between thought and feeling which manifested itself in Bernard has led, generally speaking, to a division between the contemplative and the intellectual life—so impoverishing both. In that light the great men of the next century—Dominic, Thomas Aquinas, Bonaventura, and many others—can be seen as drawing those lives together again, while in the intervening centuries there are many examples of people and movements that have achieved the primacy of being while using personality to further its ends. But such men and movements represent, it seems to me, the repairing of a break—a break all too ready to fall apart again, resulting on one side in an oppressive over-emphasis on being and on the other in the development of personality at the expense of being. In our day the reaction in monasticism to an over-emphasis on being is to allow personality enough rope with which to hang itself—which it undoubtedly will, and monasticism along with it, if the means necessary for the development of being cease to be understood.

Equally, there are signs of a reaction against living in personality, and if that is true then a development radically different from that of the last thousand years is, literally, coming into being. Bernard has been called the 'last of the Fathers' and the negative significance of this title may be that after him the capacity to understand the Bible from the standpoint of being became exceptional instead of the norm. As a result, due to the tireless activity of personality—especially from Darwin onwards—the pass has now been reached where even in a monastic milieu what is called, with pejorative overtones, a 'spiritual interpretation' is hardly, if at all, tolerated. But even if Bernard's influence can be seen as in some sense disastrous (and those whom God appoints to mediate his will always are, humanly speaking, in some sense disastrous; Darwin, just referred to, is another such example) we still, I believe, need him as much as ever, even if we must ask questions about, and attempt answers to, the problem he has left with us. For he understood the 'one thing necessary' with a marvellous clarity and urgency—no less urgent now than when he wrote:

> There are two dangers that we must guard against. We must not give to others what we have received for ourselves; nor must we keep for ourselves that which we have received to spend on others. You fall into the latter error if you possess the gift of eloquence or wisdom and yet through fear or sloth or false humility—neglect to use the gift for others' benefit. And, on the other hand, you dissipate and lose what is your own if, without right intention and from some wrong motive, you hasten to outpour yourself on others when your own soul is only half-filled.
>
> If you are wise, therefore, you will show yourself a tank and not a pipe. For a pipe pours out as fast as it takes in; but a tank waits till it is full before it overflows, and so communicates its surplus without loss to itself. We have all too few such tanks in the Church at present, though we have pipes in plenty. Of so great charity are those who mediate the heavenly waters to us that they desire to pour out when they themselves have not been inpoured; they are readier to speak than to listen, eager to teach that which they do not know, and most anxious to exercise authority on others although they have not learnt to rule themselves!

I once heard a Dominican take issue with St Bernard on the question of being a tank, his point being that God is just as pleased with pipes. Perhaps he is! Bernard continued to explain:

> But thou, my brother, whose own salvation is hardly yet assured, whose charity is feeble and unstable, if it exists at all, thou must learn not to give except when thou art full ... Be filled thyself. Then—but discreetly, mind—pour out of thy fullness. Charity, which is thus discreet as well as generous, does not waste itself by giving out but rather gains in depth ... So you see with what great graces we need

to be inpoured before we venture to give out to others—if indeed our self-giving is to be out of our fullness, not our poverty! First, we need compunction; then devotion; thirdly, the travail of repentance; fourthly, good works; fifthly, faithful prayer; sixthly, leisure for contemplation; and, in the seventh place, the fullness of love. All these things are the work in us of one and the same Spirit, according to the operation that we have called infusion; to the end that the other, which is called effusion, may be exercised with purity of heart—and therefore safely—to the praise and glory of our Lord Jesus Christ, who with the Father and the Holy Spirit liveth and reigneth, God to the ages of ages. Amen.[88]

[88] *Saint Bernard on the Song of Songs*, 44–8.

BIBLIOGRAPHY

Saint Bernard on the Song of Songs, trans., and ed. by a Religious of CSMV (A. R. Mowbray, 1952).

Henry Chadwick, *Early Christian Thought and the Classical Tradition* (Oxford University Press, 1984).

Marie-Dominique Chenu OP, *Nature, Man and Society in the Twelfth Century* (University of Chicago Press, 1968).

Michael T. Clanchy, *Abelard: A Medieval Life* (Blackwell, 1999).

Harry Nelson Coleridge, ed., *Specimens of the Table Talk of the Late Samuel Taylor Coleridge,* 2 vols. (John Murray, 1835).

Jean-Marie Déchanet, *William of St Thierry,* Cistercian Studies 10 (Cistercian Publications, 1972).

S. J. Eales, trans. and ed., *Life and Works of Saint Bernard,* 2 vols. (J. Hodges, 1896).

Etienne Gilson, *The Mystical Theology of Saint Bernard* (Sheed and Ward, 1940).

Denis Grivot and George Zarnecki, *Gislebertus: Sculptor of Autun* (Orion Press, 1961).

Anthony Hanson, 'The Struggle for the Vindication of Reason', *The Times,* 8 May 1976.

Bruno Scott James, *Saint Bernard of Clairvaux: An Essay in Biography* (Hodder & Stoughton, 1957).

Hugh Kingsmill [Lunn], *The Progress of a Biographer* (Methuen, 1949).

David Knowles, *The Evolution of Medieval Thought* (Longmans, 1962).

Jean Leclercq OSB, *The Love of Learning and the Desire for God: A Study of Monastic Culture* (Fordham University Press, 1961).

—, 'Modern Psychology and the Interpretation of Medieval Texts', *Speculum,* 48/3 (July 1973)

Dario Lisiero, *Abelard and Heloise. Between the Lines* (Lulu.com, 2012).

David E. Luscombe, ed. and trans., *Peter Abelard's Ethics: An edition with introduction, English translation and notes* (Clarendon Press, 1971).

Justin McCann OSB, ed. and trans., *The Rule of St Benedict in Latin and English* (Newman Press, 1952).

Mary McLaughlin, 'Abelard as Autobiographer: The Motives and Meaning of his *Story of Calamities*', *Speculum*, 42/3 (1967), 463–88.

Constant J. Mews, *The Lost Love Letters of Heloise and Abelard: Perceptions of Dialogue in Twelfth-Century France, with a translsation by Neville Chiavaroli and Constant J. Mews* (2nd edn Palgrave Macmillan, 2008).

A. Victor Murray, *Abelard & St Bernard* (Manchester University Press, 1967).

Peter D. Ouspensky, *In Search of the Miraculous: Fragments of an Unknown Teaching* (Routledge & Kegan Paul, 1950).

M. Basil Pennington, ed., *Bernard of Clairvaux, Studies Presented to Dom Jean Leclercq*, Cistercian Studies 23 (Cistercian Publications, 1973).

Josef Pieper, *Scholasticism: Personalities and Problems of Medieval Philosophy* (Faber & Faber, 1961).

Reginald Lane Poole, *Illustrations of the History of Medieval Thought and Learning* (1884, new edn Dover Publications, 1960).

Betty Radice, trans., ed. and introd., *The Letters of Abelard and Héloïse* (Penguin Classics, 1974).

Richard W. Southern, *Medieval Humanism and Other Studies* (Harper Torchbook, 1970).

Geoffrey Webb and Adrian Walker, trans., *St Bernard of Clairvaux: The Story of His Life as Recorded in the Vita Prima Bernardi …* (Mowbray, 1960).

P. H. Wicksteed, trans. and ed., *The Paradiso of Dante Alighieri*, Temple Classics (J. M. Dent, 1899).

Maurice Wiles, *The Remaking of Christian Doctrine* (SCM Press, 1974).

SLG PRESS PUBLICATIONS

FP1 *Prayer and the Life of Reconciliation* Gilbert Shaw (1969)
FP2 *Aloneness not Loneliness* Mother Mary Clare SLG (1969)
FP4 *Intercession* Mother Mary Clare SLG (1969)
FP8 *Prayer: Extracts from the Teaching of Father Gilbert Shaw* Gilbert Shaw (1973)
FP12 *Learning to Pray* Mother Mary Clare SLG (1970)
FP15 *Death, the Gateway to Life* Gilbert Shaw (1971, 3/2024)
FP16 *The Victory of the Cross* Dumitru Stăniloae (1970, 3/2023)
FP26 *The Message of Saint Seraphim* Irina Gorainov (1974)
FP28 *Julian of Norwich: Four Studies to Commemorate the Sixth Centenary of the Revelations of Divine Love* Sister Benedicta Ward SLG, Sister Eileen Mary SLG, Sister Mary Paul SLG, A. M. Allchin (1973, 3/2022)
FP43 *The Power of the Name: The Jesus Prayer in Orthodox Spirituality* Kallistos Ware (1974)
FP46 *Prayer and Contemplation* and *Distractions are for Healing* Robert Llewelyn (1975, 2/2024)
FP48 *The Wisdom of the Desert Fathers* trans. Sister Benedicta Ward SLG (1975)
FP50 *Letters of Saint Antony the Great* trans. Derwas Chitty (1975, 2/2021)
FP54 *From Loneliness to Solitude* Roland Walls (1976)
FP55 *Theology and Spirituality* Andrew Louth (1976, rev. 1978, 3/2024)
FP61 *Kabir: The Way of Love and Paradox* Sister Rosemary SLG (1977)
FP62 *Anselm of Canterbury: A Monastic Scholar* Sister Benedicta Ward SLG (1973, 2/2024)
FP67 *Mary and the Mystery of the Incarnation: An Essay on the Mother of God in the Theology of Karl Barth* Andrew Louth (1977, 2/2024)
FP68 *Trinity and Incarnation in Anglican Tradition* A. M. Allchin (1977, 2/2024)
FP70 *Facing Depression* Gonville ffrench-Beytagh (1978, 2/2020)
FP71 *The Single Person* Philip Welsh (1979)
FP72 *The Letters of Ammonas, Successor of St Antony* trans. Derwas Chitty, introd. Sebastian Brock (1979, 2/2023)
FP74 *George Herbert, Priest and Poet* Kenneth Mason (1980)
FP75 *A Study of Wisdom: Three Tracts by the Author of The Cloud of Unknowing* trans. Clifton Wolters (1980)
FP81 *The Psalms: Prayer Book of the Bible* Dietrich Bonhoeffer, trans. Sister Isabel SLG (1982)
FP82 *Prayer & Holiness: The Icon of Man Renewed in God* Dumitru Stăniloae (1982, rev. 2/2023)
FP85 *Walter Hilton: Eight Chapters on Perfection & Angels' Song* trans. Rosemary Dorward (1983, rev. 3/2024)
FP88 *Creative Suffering* Iulia de Beausobre (1989)
FP90 *Bringing Forth Christ: Five Feasts of the Child Jesus by St Bonaventure* trans. Eric Doyle OFM (1984, 3/2024)
FP92 *Gentleness in John of the Cross* Thomas Kane (1985)
FP94 *Saint Gregory Nazianzen: Selected Poems* trans. John McGuckin (1986, 2/2024)
FP95 *The World of the Desert Fathers: Stories and Sayings from the Anonymous Series of the Apophthegmata Patrum* trans. Columba Stewart OSB (1986, 2/2020)

FP104 *Growing Old with God* Timothy N. Rudd (1988, 2/2020)
FP106 *Julian Reconsidered* Kenneth Leech, Sister Benedicta Ward SLG (1988/ rev. 2/2024)
FP108 *The Unicorn: Meditations on the Love of God* Harry Galbraith Miller (1989)
FP109 *The Creativity of Diminishment* Sister Anke (1990)
FP110 *Called to be Priests* Hugh Wybrew (1989, updated 2/2024)
FP111 *A Kind of Watershed: An Anglican Lay View of Sacramental Confession*
Christine North (1990, updated 2/2022)
FP116 *Jesus, the Living Lord* Bishop Michael Ramsey (1992)
FP120 *The Monastic Letters of Saint Athanasius the Great*
trans. and introd. Leslie Barnard (1994, 2/2023)
FP122 *The Hidden Joy* Sister Jane SLG, ed. Dorothy Sutherland (1994)
FP124 *Prayer of the Heart: An Approach to Silent Prayer and Prayer in the Night*
Alexander Ryrie (1995, 3/2020)
FP126 *Evelyn Underhill, Anglican Mystic: Two Centenary Essays*
A. M. Allchin, Bishop Michael Ramsey (1977, 3/2024)
FP127 *Apostolate and the Mirrors of Paradox*
Sydney Evans, ed. Andrew Linzey & Brian Horne (1996)
FP128 *The Wisdom of Saint Isaac the Syrian* Sebastian Brock (1997)
FP129 *Saint Thérèse of Lisieux: Her Relevance for Today* Sister Eileen Mary SLG (1997)
FP130 *Expectations: Five Addresses for Those Beginning Ministry* Sister Edmée SLG (1997, 2/2024)
FP131 *Scenes from Animal Life: Fables for the Enneagram Types*
Waltraud Kirschke, trans. Sister Isabel SLG (1998)
FP132 *Praying the Word of God: The Use of Lectio Divina* Charles Dumont OCSO (1999)
FP133 *Love Unknown: Meditations on the Death and Resurrection of Jesus*
John Barton (1999, 2/2024)
FP134 *The Hidden Way of Love: Jean-Pierre de Caussade's Spirituality of Abandonment*
Barry Conaway (1999, 2/2024)
FP135 *Shepherd and Servant: The Spiritual Theology of Saint Dunstan* Douglas Dales (2000)
FP137 *Pilgrimage of the Heart* Sister Benedicta Ward SLG (2001)
FP138 *Mixed Life* Walter Hilton, trans. Rosemary Dorward (2001, enlarged rev. 3/2024)
FP139 *In the Footsteps of the Lord: The Teaching of Abba Isaiah of Scetis*
John Chryssavgis, Luke Penkett (2001, 2/2023)
FP140 *A Great Joy: Reflections on the Meaning of Christmas* Kenneth Mason (2001)
FP141 *Bede and the Psalter* Sister Benedicta Ward SLG (2002, 2/2024)
FP142 *Abhishiktananda: A Memoir of Dom Henri Le Saux* Murray Rogers, David Barton (2003)
FP143 *Friendship in God: The Encounter of Evelyn Underhill & Sorella Maria of Campello*
A. M. Allchin (2003, 2/2024)
FP144 *Christian Imagination in Poetry and Polity: Some Anglican Voices from Temple to Herbert*
Bishop Rowan Williams (2004)
FP145 *The Reflections of Abba Zosimas: Monk of the Palestinian Desert*
trans. and introd. John Chryssavgis (2005, 3/2022)
FP146 *The Gift of Theology: The Trinitarian Vision of Ann Griffiths and Elizabeth of Dijon*
A. M. Allchin (2005)
FP147 *Sacrifice and Spirit* Bishop Michael Ramsey (2005)
FP148 *Saint John Cassian on Prayer* trans. A. M. Casiday (2006, 2/2024)
FP149 *Hymns of Saint Ephrem the Syrian* trans. Mary Hansbury (2006, 2/2024)
FP150 *Suffering: Why All this Suffering? What Do I Do about It?*
Reinhard Körner OCD, trans. Sister Avis Mary SLG (2006)

FP151 *A True Easter: The Synod of Whitby 664 AD* Sister Benedicta Ward SLG (2007, 2/2023)

FP152 *Prayer as Self-Offering* Alexander Ryrie (2007)

FP153 *From Perfection to the Elixir: How George Herbert Fashioned a Famous Poem* Benedick de la Mare (2008, 2/2024)

FP154 *The Jesus Prayer: Gospel Soundings* Sister Pauline Margaret CHN (2008)

FP155 *Loving God Whatever: Through the Year with Sister Jane* Sister Jane SLG (2006)

FP156 *Prayer and Meditation for a Sleepless Night* SISTERS OF THE LOVE OF GOD (1993, 3/2024)

FP157 *Being There: Caring for the Bereaved* John Porter (2009)

FP158 *Learn to Be at Peace: The Practice of Stillness* Andrew Norman (2010)

FP159 *From Holy Week to Easter* George Pattison (2010)

FP160 *Strength in Weakness: The Scandal of the Cross* John W. Rogerson (2010)

FP161 *Augustine Baker: Frontiers of the Spirit* Victor de Waal (2010, 2/2024)

FP162 *Out of the Depths* Gonville ffrench-Beytagh; epilogue Wendy Robinson (1990, 2/2010)

FP163 *God and Darkness: A Carmelite Perspective* Gemma Hinricher OCD, trans. Sister Avis Mary SLG (2010)

FP164 *The Gift of Joy* Curtis Almquist SSJE (2011)

FP165 *'I Have Called You Friends': Suggestions for the Spiritual Life Based on the Farewell Discourses of Jesus* Reinhard Körner OCD (2012)

FP166 *Leisure* Mother Mary Clare SLG (2012)

FP167 *Carmelite Ascent: An Introduction to Saint Teresa and Saint John of the Cross* Mother Mary Clare SLG (1973, rev. 2012)

FP168 *Ann Griffiths and Her Writings* Llewellyn Cumings (2012)

FP169 *The Our Father* Sister Benedicta Ward SLG (2012)

FP171 *The Spiritual Wisdom of the Syriac Book of Steps* Robert A. Kitchen (2013)

FP172 *The Prayer of Silence* Alexander Ryrie (2012)

FP173 *On Tour in Byzantium: Excerpts from The Spiritual Meadow of John Moschus* Ralph Martin SSM (2013)

FP174 *Monastic Life* Bonnie Thurston (2016)

FP175 *Shall All Be Well? Reflections for Holy Week* Graham Ward (2015)

FP176 *Solitude and Communion: Papers on the Hermit Life* ed. A. M. Allchin (2015)

FP177 *The Prayers of Jacob of Serugh* ed. Mary Hansbury (2015)

FP178 *The Monastic Hours of Prayer* Sister Benedicta Ward SLG (2016)

FP179 *The Desert of the Heart: Daily Readings with the Desert Fathers* trans. Sister Benedicta Ward SLG (2016)

FP180 *In Company with Christ: Lent, Palm Sunday, Good Friday & Easter to Pentecost* Sister Benedicta Ward SLG (2016)

FP181 *Lazarus: Come Out! Reflections on John 11* Bonnie Thurston (2017)

FP182 *Unknowing & Astonishment: Meditations on Faith for the Long Haul* Christopher Scott (2018)

FP183 *Pondering, Praying, Preaching: Romans 8* Bonnie Thurston (2019, 2/2021)

FP184 *Shem`on the Graceful: Discourse on the Solitary Life* trans. and introd. Mary Hansbury (2020)

FP185 *God Under My Roof: Celtic Songs and Blessings* Esther de Waal (2020)

FP186 *Journeying with the Jesus Prayer* James F. Wellington (2020)

FP187 *Poet of the Word: Re-reading Scripture with Ephraem the Syrian* Aelred Partridge OC (2020)

FP188 *Identity and Ritual* Alan Griffiths (2021)
FP189 *River of the Spirit: The Spirituality of Simon Barrington-Ward* Andy Lord (2021)
FP190 *Prayer and the Struggle against Evil* John Barton, Daniel Lloyd, James Ramsay, Alexander Ryrie (2021)
FP191 *Dante's Spiritual Journey: A Reading of the Divine Comedy* Tony Dickinson (2021)
FP192 *Jesus the Undistorted Image of God* John Townroe (2022)
FP193 *Our Deepest Desire: Prayer, Fasting & Almsgiving in the Writings of Saint Augustine of Hippo* Sister Susan SLG (2022)
FP194 *Lent with George Herbert* Tony Dickinson (2022)
FP195 *Four Ways to the Cross* Tony Dickinson (2022)
FP196 *Anselm of Canterbury, Teacher of Prayer* Sister Benedicta Ward SLG (2022)
FP197 *With One Heart and Mind: Prayers out of Stillness* Anthony Kemp (2023)
FP198 *Sayings of the Urban Fathers & Mothers* James Ashdown (2023)
FP199 *Doors* Sister Raphael SLG (2023)
FP200 *Monastic Vocation* SISTERS OF THE LOVE OF GOD, Bishop Rowan Williams (2021)
FP201 *An Ecology of the Heart: Faith Through the Climate Crisis* Duncan Forbes (2023)
FP202 *'In the image of the Image': Gregory of Nyssa's Opposition to Slavery* Adam Couchman (2023)
FP203 *Gregory of Nyssa and the Sins of Asia Minor* Jonathan Farrugia (2023)
FP204 *Discovery* Arthur Bell (2023)
FP205 *Living Healing: the Spirituality of Leanne Payne* Andy Lord (2023)
FP206 *Still Listening: Sowing the Seeds of the Jesus Prayer* Bruce Batstone CJN (2023)
FP207 *Julian of Norwich: Four Essays to Commemorate 650 Years of the Revelations of Divine Love* Bishop Graham Usher, Father Colin CSWG, Sister Elizabeth Ruth Obbard OC, Mother Hilary Crupi OJN (2023)
FP208 *TIME* Dumitru Stăniloae, Kallistos Ware (2023)
FP209 *Pearls of Life: A Lifebelt for the Spirit* Tony Dickinson (2024)
FP210 *The Way and the Truth and the Life: An Exploration by a Follower of the Way* James Ramsay (2024)
FP211 *Cosmos, Crisis & Christ: Essays of Wendy Robinson* Wendy Robinson (2024)
FP212 *Towards a Theology of Psychotherapy: The Spirituality of Wendy Robinson* Andrew Louth (2024)
FP213 *Immersed in God and the World: Living Priestly Ministry* Andy Lord (2024)
FP214 *The Road to Emmaus: A Sculptor's Journey through Time* Rodney Munday (2024)
FP215 *Prayer Too Deep for Words* Sister Edmée SLG (2024)
FP216 *The Prayers of St Isaac of Nineveh* Sebastian Brock (2024)
FP217 *Two Medieval English Saints: Cuthbert and Alban* Sister Benedicta Ward SLG (2024)
FP218 *Encountering the Depths* Mother Mary Clare SLG (1981, rev. 3/2024)
FP219 *Conflict and Concord* Sister Susan SLG, Bishop Humphrey Southern, Bronwen Neil, Sister Rosemary SLG, Sister Clare-Louise SLG (2024)
FP220 *Divine Love in the Song of Songs* Sister Edmée SLG (2024)
FP221 *Zeal for the Faith: An Introduction to Christian-Muslim Dialogue* Tony Dickinson (2024)
FP222 *Bernard & Abelard* Sister Edmée SLG (2024)
FP223 *Eliot's Transitions: T. S. Eliot's Search for Identity and the Society of the Sacred Mission at Kelham Hall* Vincent Strudwick (2024)

Contemplative Poetry series

CP1	*Amado Nervo: Poems of Faith and Doubt*	trans. John Gallas (2021)
CP2	*Anglo-Saxon Poets: The High Roof of Heaven*	trans. John Gallas (2021)
CP3	*Middle English Poets: Where Grace Grows Ever Green*	ed. John Gallas (2021)
CP4	*Selected Poems: The Voice inside Our Home*	Edward Clarke (2022)
CP5	*Women & God: Drops in the Sea of Time*	trans. and ed. John Gallas (2022)
CP6	*Gabrielle de Coignard & Vittoria Colonna: Fly Not Too High*	trans. John Gallas (2022)
CP7	*Selected Poems: Chancing on Sanctity*	James Ramsay (2022)
CP8	*Gabriela Mistral: This Far Place*	trans. John Gallas (2023)
CP9	*Henry Vaughan & George Herbert: Divine Themes and Celestial Praise*	ed. Edward Clarke (2023)
CP10	*Love Will Come with Fire*	Sisters of the Love of God (2023)
CP11	*Touchpapers*	coll. and trans. John Gallas (2023)
CP12	*Seasons of my Soul*	Clare McKerron (2023)
CP13	*Reinhard Sorge: Take Flight to God*	trans. John Gallas (2024)
CP14	*Embertide: Encountering Saint Frideswide*	Romola Parish (2024)
CP15	*Thomas Campion: Made All of Light*	ed. and introd. Julia Craig-McFeely (2024)

Vestry Guides

VG1	*The Visiting Minister: How to Welcome Visiting Clergy to Your Church*	Paul Monk (2021)
VG2	*Help! No Minister! or Please Take the Service*	Paul Monk (2022)
VG3	*The Liturgy of the Eucharist: An Introductory Guide*	Paul Monk (2024)

www.slgpress.co.uk

The Sisters of the Love of God is an Anglican community of women religious living a contemplative monastic life.

To learn more about the Community and the Convent of the Incarnation at Fairacres, Oxford, see our website www.slg.org.uk.

As well as supporting those seeking to follow a vocation to the monastic life, the Community has a number of forms of association for those who feel drawn to share in the Sisters' life of prayer: Fellowship of the Love of God, Companions, Priests Associate or Oblate Sisters.

For more information email sisters@slg.org.uk or write to The Reverend Mother, Convent of the Incarnation, Parker Street, Oxford, OX4 1TB, UK.